MASTERING COREL PAINTSHOP PRO

Your Comprehensive Beginners Guide to Master the Use of Corel PaintShop Pro

EMILY SMITH

Copyright © 2024 by EMILY SMITH

All Right Reserved

This material is protected by intellectual property regulations. Any duplication, archiving in a retrieval system, or dissemination in any format or by any means, including digital, mechanical, xerographic, recording, or other techniques, is strictly forbidden without prior written consent from the publisher, except as permitted by United States copyright law and fair use.

Disclaimer and Terms of Use

Although the writer and publisher have carefully ensured the correctness, relevance, suitability, and completeness of this publication and its supplementary materials, they offer no guarantees or assurances regarding its content. The details provided are meant solely for informational purposes. If you decide to apply the principles outlined in this book, you do so at your own risk and bear full responsibility for your actions.

Printed in the United States of America.

TABLE OF CONTENTS

TABLE OF CONTENTS iii

INTRODUCTION 1

CHAPTER ONE 2

WHAT'S NEW IN COREL PAINTSHOP PRO 2

    WHAT EXACTLY IS COREL? 3

    FEATURES OF COREL PAINTSHOP PRO 3

    WORKSPACE CHANGES 4

    GETTING STARTED WITH PAINTSHOP PRO 4

    64-BIT AND 32-BIT INSTALLATION OPTIONS 5

    HOW TO DOWNLOAD COREL PAINTSHOP PRO 5

    HOW TO USE THE FRAME TOOL 8

    BASIC PHOTO CORRECTION IN PAINTSHOP PRO 8

    CROPPING IMAGES 10

    AI BACKGROUND REPLACEMENT 11

    AI PORTRAIT MODE 12

CHAPTER TWO 13

WORKSPACE 13

    TOURING THE WORKSPACE 13

    WORKSPACE TABS 13

        Welcome Tab 14

        Manage Tab 15

        Edit Tab 16

    CUSTOMIZABLE TABS: ADJUST (FULL WORKSPACE) 17

Changing Between Tabs	19
Switching Between Various Workspaces	19
Switch Workspaces Efficiently	19
PHOTOGRAPHY WORKSPACE	*20*
TOOLS TAILORED FOR YOUR PHOTOGRAPHY WORKSPACE	*21*
AI FEATURES IN PHOTOGRAPHY WORKSPACE	*21*
CHOOSE A COLOR SCHEME FOR YOUR WORKSPACE	*21*
How to Adjust the Color of Your Background	22
USING PALETTES	*22*
Show a Palette	25
Resizing a Palette	25
WORKING WITH THE VARIOUS TOOLBARS	*25*
How can the Visibility of a Toolbar be Toggled?	26
Use the Tools at your Disposal	26
ADJUST YOUR PALETTES AND TOOLBARS	*31*
HOW TO SET UP YOUR PREFERRED DOCKING METHOD	*31*
How to Dock a Toolbar or Palette	31
How to Float a Toolbar or Palette and Achieve it	31
How to Move a Palette or a Toolbar within an Application	32
Raise a Toolbar or Palette	32
WORKING WITH DIALOG BOXES	*33*
Using the Preview Areas Efficiently	33
GUIDANCE FOR ZOOMING IN AND OUT OF THE PICTURE PREVIEW	*34*
How to Pan a Preview Image	34
Proof Changes in the Main Image Window	35
How to Professionally Edit the Numeric Values	35
How to Select a Color from your Dialog Box	35
Modify Settings in a Dialog Box at Random.	35
HOW TO VIEW YOUR IMAGES	*36*
Turn the Tabbed Image Window Option on or Off	36

Optimize the Size of the Image Window.. 37
Close the Image Window 38
How can I Duplicate the image Currently on the Screen?...................... 38
Arranging Multiple Windows on Your Screen 38
To Examine a Different Section of the Image... 38
Adjust the Image to fit within the Image Window 39

USING KEYBOARD SHORTCUTS FOR ENHANCED EFFICIENCY....................... 39

HOW TO ACCESS A DETAILED LIST OF ALL AVAILABLE CONTEXT MENUS 39
Guidelines for Utilizing a Context-Accessible Menu 40

GRID 41
What are Grids?... 41
What are Guides? 41
Adjusting the Snapping Feature... 41

SETTING RULER PROPERTIES 41
Exploring Grid Properties and how to Customize them 42

SET UP A VERTICAL OR HORIZONTAL GUIDE 43
Guidelines for Adjusting the Color of a Guide.. 44

ADDING IMAGES TO COREL PAINTSHOP PRO 44

GUIDELINES FOR UPLOADING IMAGES IN PAINTSHOP PRO 45
Establishing Connections with Multiple Image Scanners........................ 45

SAVING IMAGES 45

HOW TO PROPERLY SAVE A NEW IMAGE 47

CHAPTER THREE 49

COREL RAW IMAGES 49

RAW IMAGE IN PAINTSHOP PRO 49

PUT CAMERA RAW LAB TO USE 50
Launch the Camera RAW Lab... 51
Adjust RAW Images Settings.. 52

v

Adjust Several RAW Images 53

HOW TO CONVERT IMAGES TAKEN IN RAW FORMAT TO ANOTHER FORMAT *53*

How to Convert a RAW Picture to a Different File Type? 53
Use XMP files to Carry out your Tasks 54
Read and Import Metadata in XMP Files 54
Save Changes in XMP Files 54

CHAPTER FOUR 56

TRANSFERRING AND RETOUCHING PHOTOS 56

HOW TO TRANSFER IMAGES TO DIFFERENT APPLICATIONS *56*

DUPLICATE YOUR IMAGES FOR USE IN VARIOUS APPLICATIONS *56*

HOW TO ZOOM AND PAN *57*

How to Zoom 57
How to Zoom in On a Section of an Image... 58
How to Pan Around Your Image 59
How to Undo and Redo Your Changes 60
Controls for Redo and Undo are Located on the History Palette 60
Undo an Action 61
Redo an Action 62
Use the History Palette to Undo and Redo Actions 62
Adjust your Undo Settings 63

HOW TO REPEAT A COMMAND *64*

USING ADJUST *65*

What does the Adjust tab Signify? 65
Activate the Adjust Tab 65
Access the Adjust Tab in your Browser 66
Revert Modifications in the Adjust Section 66
Using Depth Info to Choose Areas 66

SELECT A POINT BASED ON THE DEPTH OF INFO *67*

- MANAGE TAB 67
  - Switch Effortlessly Between Preview and Thumbnail Modes 67
  - Adjust the Size of the Manage Tab Palettes 68
- HIDE OR DISPLAY THE NAVIGATION PALETTE AND INFORMATION PALETTE 68
- BROWSE FOLDERS FOR YOUR IMAGES 68
  - How to Access the Images in a Folder 69
  - Add a New Folder to the Collection Page 70
  - Remove the Folder from the Collection Page 70
- LOCATE IMAGES ON YOUR PC 71
- CONDUCT A QUICK SEARCH FOR IMAGES 71
- PERFORMING AN ADVANCED SEARCH 71

CHAPTER FIVE 73

PHOTO PERSPECTIVE AND LENS CORRECTION 73

- CORRECTING PHOTOGRAPHIC PERSPECTIVE 73
- HOW TO CORRECT PERSPECTIVE IN PHOTOS 73
  - Precise Perspective in the Image Layer 74
- HOW TO MAKE BASIC CHANGES TO THE IMAGE USING MECHANICAL TOOLS 75
- HOW TO CORRECT ANY ISSUES USING SMART PHOTO FIX 75
- HOW TO USE THE ADVANCED FEATURES OF THE SMART PHOTO FIX 77
- LIGHTEN IMAGES 78
  - How to Bring out the Best in your Images 78
- DARKEN IMAGES 79
  - How to Darken Your Image 79
- REMOVING THE PURPLE RUFFLES 79
- ELIMINATING DIGITAL NOISE 80

- *REMOVING DIGITAL NOISE COMMAND* 81
- *RAPIDLY REMOVING DIGITAL NOISE* 81
  - Use AI Denoise for Noise Analysis and Removal 81
- *HOW TO PROTECT IMAGE AREAS FROM NOISE CORRECTIONS* 83
- *DELETE CHROMATIC ABERRATIONS IN THE IMAGE* 83
- *REMOVE CHROMATIC ABERRATIONS IN YOUR PHOTOS* 84
- *DISTORTION* 85
- *VIGNETTING* 86
- *USING LENS CORRECTION* 88
  - Exploring Various Forms of Lens Distortion 88
  - Correcting Barrel Distortion 89
  - Correcting the Fish-eye Distortion 89
  - Correct the Pincushion Distortion 89

CHAPTER SIX 90

WHITE BALANCE 90

- *HOW TO ADJUST WHITE BALANCE* 90
- *HOW TO MIX COLOR CHANNELS* 91
  - Restore the Colors that have Lost their Vibrancy 92
  - How to Adjust the Color Cast 93
  - Adjust the Contrast, Brightness, and Clarity. 93
- *HISTOGRAMS* 94
  - Make Adjustments to either the Contrast or the Brightness 95
  - Lighten up the Dark Areas and the Clarity 96
  - Enhancing Both the Depth and the Clarity 96
  - How to Modify the Brightness of the Color Channels 97
- *HOW TO ADJUST THE MID-TONES, HIGHLIGHTS, AND SHADOWS* 99
  - How to Correct Exposure by Using a Histogram 99
  - Expanding the Histogram and Contrast 101

CHAPTER SEVEN 102

HUE AND SATURATION 102

   HOW TO ADJUST THE HUE AND SATURATION 102

   HOW TO CREATE A DUO-TONE IMAGE 104

   ADJUST THE LIGHTING, COLOR, AND SATURATION 104

      Adjust the Colors 106

   HOW TO REMOVE AND ADJUST THE NOISE 107

      How to Add Noise 109

      Removing more Weave Patterns 110

      Remove Individual Pixel Spots 111

      How to Remove Multi-pixel Specks 111

   REMOVING DISTRACTIONS WHILE PRESERVING THE AUTHENTIC TEXTURES 112

   CHOOSE A SPECIFIC AREA OF FOCUS 113

      How to Adjust Blurred Areas 113

   SET UP A FOCUS AREA USING THE FIELD OF DEPTH EFFECT 113

   HOW TO BLUR IMAGES 114

      Why would Someone Blur an Image? 115

   HOW TO SHARPEN IMAGES 115

      Enhance the Level of Sharpness you Apply 117

      How to use both low and high-frequency sharpening techniques 117

   SOFTEN IMAGES 118

   WHAT OCCURS WITH PIXELS DURING IMAGE RESAMPLING? 118

   ARE THERE ALTERNATIVE TECHNIQUES AVAILABLE FOR RESIZING IMAGES? 119

   HOW TO RESIZE IMAGES 120

   USING UPSAMPLING POWERED BY AI TO MAKE YOUR IMAGES LARGER .. 122

   INCREASING IMAGE SIZE THROUGH AI-POWERED UPSAMPLING 123

HOW TO WORK WITH COLORS AND MATERIALS.. 124

USING THE MATERIALS PALETTE IN PAINTSHOP ULTIMATE 124

SELECT COLORS FROM THE DESKTOP OR AN IMAGE................................. 125
    Using the Eyedropper Tool allows you to Select Colors from the Image you are currently working on.. 125

USE THE DROPPER TOOL TO SELECT COLORS AND FILL AND SAMPLE ACCORDINGLY 126
    Select your Colors from the Desktop 126

CHAPTER EIGHT 127

GRADIENT AND PATTERNS 127

USING GRADIENTS.. 127

HOW TO APPLY YOUR CURRENT GRADIENT 128
    How to Save Edited Gradients 128
    How to Create Gradients 128
    Change the Names of Gradients 129
    Remove Gradients 129
    Editing Gradients 129

ADJUSTING THE MIDPOINTS OR MARKERS 130
    How to Add Markers.. 130
    Changing the Color of a Marker... 130
    Adjusting the Midpoints or Markers 131

ADJUST GRADIENTS ON VECTOR OBJECTS AND INSTANTLY SEE THE CHANGES... 131
    Exporting and Importing Gradients 132
    Exporting Gradients 132
    How to Import GRD Gradients 132

USING PATTERNS.. 132

HOW TO SELECT PATTERNS 133
    How to use a Selection or an Active Image as a Pattern 134

USING TEXTURES 134
    Apply Current Texture 134
    How to Select a Texture 134

HOW TO SAVE PHOTOS AS TEXTURES 136

USING SWATCHES AND CUSTOM COLOR PALETTES 136
    Swatches 137
    Select Color Palettes 137
    Creating Palettes 138
    How to Import a Swatch Palette 138
    Create Swatches 138
    Selecting a Swatch 139
    Renaming Swatches 139
    Changing the Display of Swatches 139

CHAPTER NINE 141

TIPS, TRICKS AND TROUBLESHOOTING 141

TIPS AND TRICKS 141

CUSTOMIZE YOUR WORKSPACE 141

USE SHORTCUTS ON THE KEYBOARD 142

MASTER SELECTION TOOLS 142

CHECK OUR ADJUSTMENT LAYERS 143

ACQUIRE KNOWLEDGE OF LAYER MASKING TECHNIQUES 144

USE SMART SELECTION TOOLS 144

USE TEMPLATES AND PRESETS THAT ARE AVAILABLE 145

TRY OUT DIFFERENT FILTERS AND EFFECTS 145

USE PLUGINS TO ACCESS ADDITIONAL FUNCTIONALITY 146

ENGAGE IN NON-DESTRUCTIVE EDITING 147

TROUBLESHOOTING PAINTSHOP PRO 147

SYSTEM REQUIREMENTS 148

TYPICAL PROBLEMS AND POSSIBLE SOLUTIONS 148

    Performance Problems 148

    Freezing or Crashing 148

    Brush or Tool Problems 149

    Problems with the Workspace or the Interface 150

    Issues with the File Compatibility 150

    Activation or Licensing Document Difficulties 151

    Problems with the Printing Process 151

    Management Color Issues 152

CHAPTER TEN **154**

WORKING WITH EFFECTS **154**

  CHOOSING EFFECTS 154

  USE THE INSTANT EFFECTS PALETTE 155

  USE THE EFFECT BROWSER 155

  EMPLOY 3D EFFECTS 156

  USE BUTTONIZE 156

  USE CHISEL 157

  MASTERING THE DROP SHADOW 157

    Using the Inner Bevel 158

    Using Outer Bevel 160

    Using Brush Strokes 161

    Using Charcoal 162

    Using Colored Pencil 162

    Using Pencil 163

CONCLUSION **164**

INDEX **165**

INTRODUCTION

Corel PaintShop Pro facilitates the creation of visually enticing compositions and noteworthy design projects. This latest iteration provides PaintShop Pro with enhanced speed, power, user-friendliness, and creative capabilities. Enhance the luminosity of your photographs with increased AI power and practical tools to achieve results as unique as your photographs themselves. PaintShop Pro consistently enhances the vibrancy of your digital environment. PaintShop Pro is an advanced photo editor that provides a versatile selection of graphic design and editing tools suitable for professionals, in addition to AI-based solutions that help save time.

Using Corel PaintShop Pro , specific regions of an image can be easily cropped out. The straightforward options for resizing an image are presets, pixels, percentages, and print scale, faded photographs by restoring and repairing them with tools such as the Scratch Remover and Fade Correction, which improve contrast and color. In addition, the search toolbar can be utilized to locate various tools, thereby enhancing work productivity and saving time. Using AI Upsampling, it is possible to enlarge an image without introducing undesirable distortion. Photographs can be embellished with artistic effects by employing AI Style Transfer. Due to the icon that is prominently showcased on them, tools are remarkably identifiable. The user-friendly interface of this software renders it effortless to operate.

CHAPTER ONE

WHAT'S NEW IN COREL PAINTSHOP PRO

PaintShop Pro includes three entirely new features: Snap to Objects, AfterShot Lab, and Focus Stacking (more on these new features in a moment). The update has additionally improved or enhanced the Frame Tool, the prototype of the real-time composite mode, and overall performance and usability. The final one features a redesigned New from Template page with improved categorization and filtering capabilities. Additionally, "30% performance improvement when using Refine Brush" is touted by the manufacturer. Additional software included with the Ultimate edition, such as Painter Essentials 8 and MultiCam Capture Lite 2, has also been improved.

Corel invests a great deal of effort in enhancing and adding features to the venerable image editing software, determining user preferences through program telemetry and user advisory forums. AI Background Replacement, AI Portrait Mode, AI Style Transfer, and support for the HEIC and HEIF file formats utilized by iPhones are among the most recent enhancements. An extensive array of features has been introduced, including picture tubes, patterns, color palettes, brushes, and a Frame tool that enables the placement of images within shapes.

WHAT EXACTLY IS COREL?

In the domains of design and editing, Corel is widely acknowledged as a leading brand. It is a brand of editing software that enables the editing of digital photographs and videos through the use of extraordinary editing capabilities. The organization supplies instruments of superior quality that are equipped with an extensive array of exceptional attributes. Multiple objects designed for photo editing are provided by the organization for your convenience. Certain videos and images can be altered without the need for prior expertise in design or editing.

A comprehensive comparison of Corel PaintShop Pro and Ultimate is available for those interested in learning more about the two variants. Corel PaintShop is available in two distinct versions. This article will analyze the Pro version of the aforementioned program, which has been upgraded. Corel Paintshop Pro is equipped with an abundance of improved tools and features that facilitate and encourage artistic expression through the process of image modification.

FEATURES OF COREL PAINTSHOP PRO

As an enhancement, the most recent release of Corel Paintshop Pro incorporates many new tools and capabilities. A limited number of them are enumerated as follows:

- Workspace Changes.
- Content-Aware Cloning.
- Refined Selection Tool.

WORKSPACE CHANGES

Photography Workspace is a newly added feature in the most recent release of Paintshop Pro. The operation of this function does not require a touch interface. The Corel Paintshop Pro Software is designed to cater primarily to individuals who are new to the program and strive for exceptional usability. It comprises a collection of photo-editing applications that facilitate rapid modification of images. This utility facilitates the modification of photographs that are frequently utilized for sharing images from a mobile device, including a smartphone or tablet. An icon within this software contains numerous editing functions, including a crop tool, a collection of attractive filters that can be applied with a single click, and rudimentary exposure and color correction options.

New users will be capable of rapidly modifying their images by utilizing this cutting-edge photo editing application. Moreover, they will have the opportunity to advance to the more intricate Essentials or Complete workspaces. In addition, a tablet-compatible version is made available to PlayStation Portable (PSP) users who alter images frequently on a desktop computer. Every member of your family can utilize this editing program, irrespective of their level of expertise in its operation.

GETTING STARTED WITH PAINTSHOP PRO

Windows 11 or 64-bit Windows 10 (version 1903 or later with the most recent service pack) is supported by PaintShop Pro. No macOS version exists.

Before proceeding, a brief downloader program is installed to finalize the installation process. You must decide between 32-bit and 64-bit versions or both; selecting the latter option ensures compatibility with plug-ins for both 32-bit and 64-bit systems. Additionally, English, Traditional Chinese, German, Spanish, French, Italian, Japanese, or Dutch are among the eight available languages. To establish an account, the program requests an email address; further action is taken via an automatically generated confirmation email.

64-BIT AND 32-BIT INSTALLATION OPTIONS

Utilize the Installer to master the installation and removal of Corel applications for a streamlined experience. Before starting the implementation procedure, it is critical to thoroughly contemplate several essential aspects. Before beginning, ensure that all other applications are closed to prevent interruptions during the installation process. Additionally, antiviral and firewall software should be taken into account, as they can affect the installation procedure. To ensure the installation runs efficiently, ensure that you are logged in with a user account that possesses local administrative permissions or as the computer's administrator.

You have the option to install Corel applications such as PaintShop Pro in either 32-bit or 64-bit format. Although PaintShop Pro can be installed on 64-bit operating systems, users should opt for PaintShop Pro 64-bit to ensure optimal performance and access to all features. Conversely, to ensure compatibility with prior plug-ins and software, the 32-bit version is provided. The applications are enumerated and activated independently from the Windows Start menu or Start screen when both versions are installed.

HOW TO DOWNLOAD COREL PAINTSHOP PRO

PaintShop Pro is compatible with minimal system requirements and is available for both Windows and Mac. Simply obtain and install the software to begin taking advantage of its thrilling features and functions.

Among the phases are the following:

1. Start by closing all currently open programs.

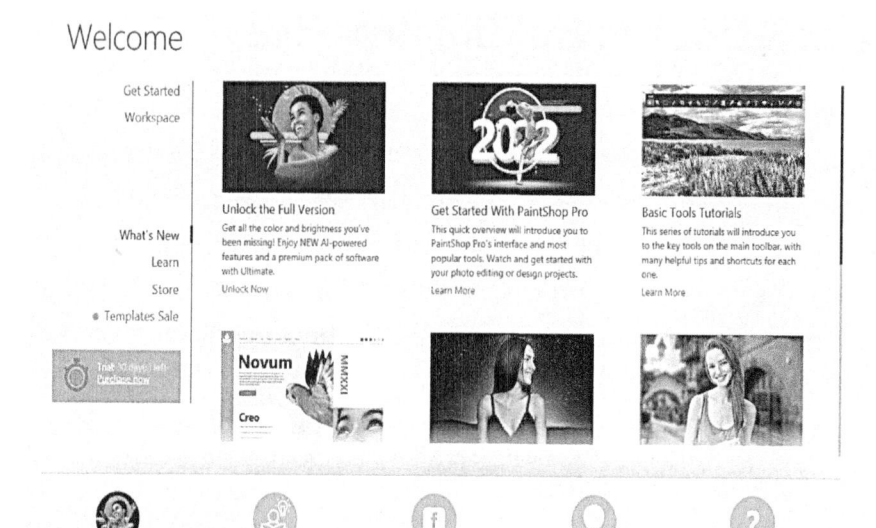

2. Insert the DVD into the DVD device or double-click the downloaded.exe file to initiate it. Manually navigate to the DVD device and double-click Setup.exe if the DVD setup application fails to activate automatically.

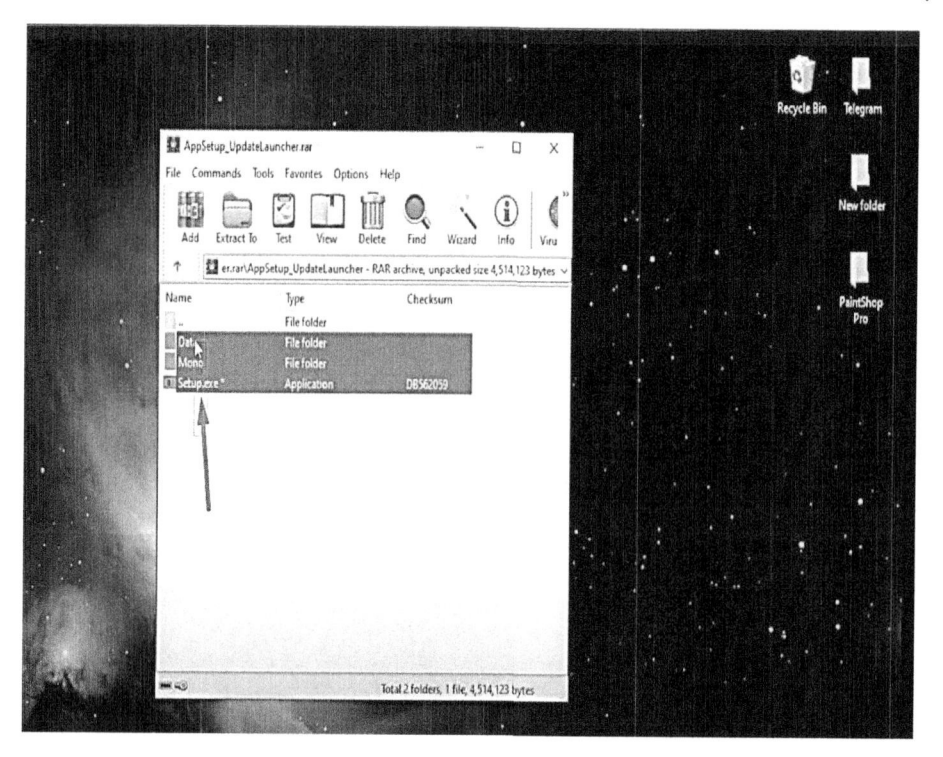

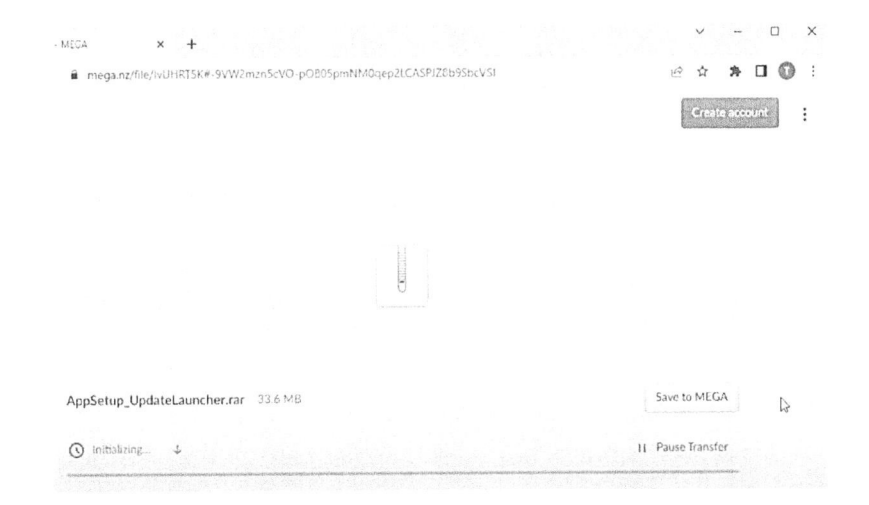

3. To complete the installation procedure successfully, adhere to the on-screen instructions.

Instructions for uninstallation:

- Launch the Control Panel for Windows.

- Select "**Uninstall a program**" from the Programs category by clicking the corresponding link.

- In the program list, locate Corel PaintShop Pro and select "**Change**" or "**Uninstall**."

- To complete uninstalling the program, simply adhere to the on-screen instructions.

HOW TO USE THE FRAME TOOL

Regardless of their level of expertise, PaintShop Pro users can effortlessly generate digital layouts and composite images using the Frame tool. Frames, which are also known as clipping filters, can be generated from vector text and any vector shape, including ellipse, rectangle, symmetric, and preset shapes. Text and vector shapes that already exist can be transformed into frames as well. You can accomplish the desired effect by filling a frame with a photograph, pattern, or hues after it has been created.

In PaintShop Pro , improvements were made to the Frame tool that debuted in PaintShop Pro 2022. It can be found in the Complete and Essentials workspaces. To view any of the images in their entirety, please click on them.

Work in the Sea-to-Sky or Photography workspace; otherwise, a workspace change is required. To access the Welcome screen, click the Home icon. From the menu on the left, select Workspace, then click Apply after selecting either the Essentials or Complete workspace. In this guide, the complete workspace is being utilized.

Note: that the Frame tool is not automatically included in the Tools toolbar when used in the Essentials workspace. To add it, simply add it to the toolbar. At the bottom of the toolbar, click the Customize (plus) icon and mark the Frame Tool checkbox.

Frame-related operations should be conducted with the Layers palette open. To enable Layers, press F8 or navigate to the Palettes menu if yours is not already visible.

BASIC PHOTO CORRECTION IN PAINTSHOP PRO

In addition to auto-correction, PaintShop Pro provides utilities such as a histogram with controls for illumination and color. Lighting issues in a number of my test photographs were remedied by the One Step Photo Fix, which is accessible in all editing workspaces. The Smart Photo Fix dialog provides significantly more functionality. To adjust the white balance, select a neutral point and utilize the Levels slider to balance an asymmetric histogram, respectively.

In addition to displaying before and after views, Smart Photo Fix allows you to observe the outcomes of your alterations and adjustments. Additionally, a Revert option is located beneath the corrections panel. Ultimately, there are instances when an excessive number of adjustments have been made to a photograph and the user desires to begin again. Forward and back controls are also useful.

While PaintShop's Effects menu deviates significantly from the well-known options found on Instagram, it does provide Instant Effects that emulate those. Using the Time Machine function, one can visualize the appearance of a given photograph from 1839 to 1960. An extensive variety of effects are available, including artistic, film, B&W, and scene illumination. When you select an effect, a preview of it appears alongside the original image.

An additional deficiency pertains to the absence of regulation over the consequences. Occasionally, one can desire to slightly diminish the intensity, as I discovered in the case of the Instant Film effect. The immediate effects in Photoshop Elements are customizable, whereas those in PaintShop are not.

CROPPING IMAGES

Crop tools are by far the most frequently used photo modification tools. Although seemingly inconsequential, Adobe significantly enhanced the crop tool in Photoshop, even incorporating AI-driven auto-suggested cropping, which is now available in Photoshop Elements as well. Additionally, Corel continues to develop its crop tool. It improves your perception of the final product by reducing the brightness of the surrounding area. It provides composition guide overlays, such as the rule of thirds, golden spiral, and golden ratio. The crop box remains in place during tool rotation, allowing you to observe the result without having to tilt your head.

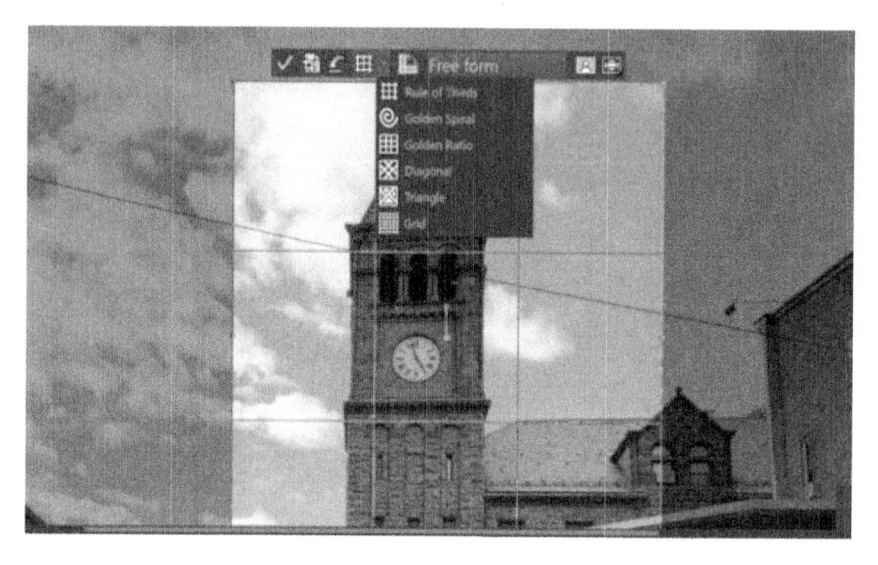

These overlays surpass those of Adobe Photoshop Elements, which rotates the crop box rather than the image and lacks certain elements (such as the golden spiral). However, Elements includes some interesting cookie-cutter crops, such as animal and heart shapes, and Adobe's cropping tools feel more precise and responsive in general than Corel's.

AI BACKGROUND REPLACEMENT

Changing the background of a photo in Photoshop was formerly a hit-or-miss endeavor requiring multiple steps. In that regard, both that program and PaintShop have reversed the procedure, reducing the process to a single click. In addition to working with human subjects, the AI Background Replacement tool in PaintShop and Skylum Luminar now offers tools for editing the backgrounds of landscapes. The latter component remains absent from PaintShop.

The AI Background replacement feature is comparable to the Subject Select tool in Photoshop. This tool allows you to easily replace the background layer while immediately isolating and masking a human (or nonhuman) subject in your image. Nevertheless, PaintShop streamlines the procedure by providing pre-established backgrounds.

This utility is located ninth from the top of the Adjust > Artificial Intelligence menu. Why it is located there as opposed to in the Enhance Photo, Edit, Image, or Effects menu is beyond my comprehension. Could an AI Tools interface be of assistance? Please note that the utility is not accessible within the Photography workspace. It performed almost flawlessly during testing by selecting me from a photograph with a landscape background. Additionally, you can refine, add to, and erase a selected area using a brush. To assess the quality of the selection, you are presented with various view options, such as transparent checkerboard, white, or black.

AI PORTRAIT MODE

I had anticipated AI face manipulation capabilities comparable to those found in ON1 and Photoshop; however, the AI Portrait Mode merely permits subject selection and background blurring. It operates similarly to the Portrait mode on the iPhone. The preciseness of selection determines the caliber of the outcome. My test picture of the selection was less than ideal, but fortunately, that is something that can be adjusted. Considering that the effect simulates lens bokeh, the option between round and hexagonal apertures is intriguing. It was most effective to utilize the latter with reduced feathering.

CHAPTER TWO

WORKSPACE

TOURING THE WORKSPACE

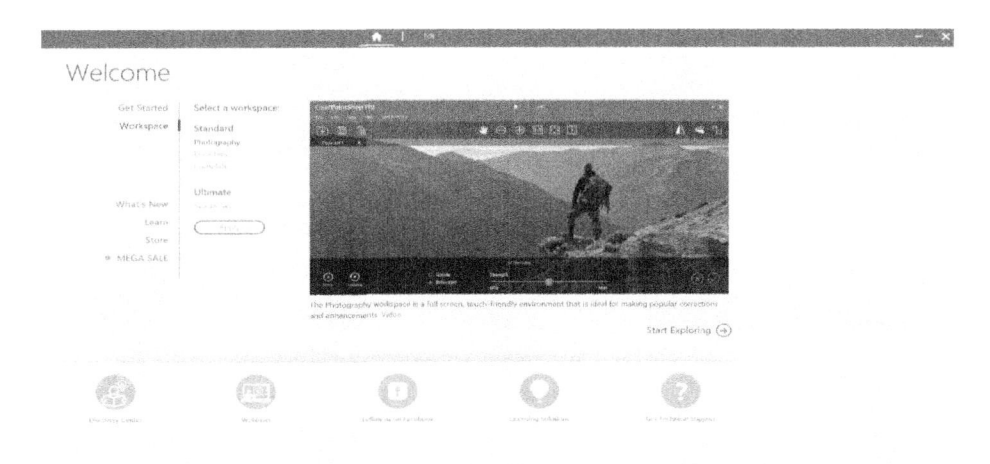

Three primary workspaces are available in PaintShop Pro: Photography, Essentials, and Complete. The comprehensive PaintShop Pro workspace grants users access to all instruments required for a variety of tasks. The Essentials workspace features an orderly and aesthetically pleasing arrangement and is furnished with a minimal array of tools. The photography work environment offers touchscreen-optimized, intuitive image modification.

In addition to the preconfigured workspaces, users are provided with the choice to construct and save a custom workspace or select a specialized workspace.

WORKSPACE TABS

Utilize sections to arrange information and features. The Photography, Essentials, and Complete workspaces each have their own set of default tabs.

- Welcome to the comprehensive editions, photography, and essentials.

- Manage
- Editing capabilities are extended to Photography, Essentials, and Complete, with adjustments made following the preferences of each workspace.
- The Adjust tab is a feature of the complete suite and is not the default.

Utilize the tools and controls accessible via each tab to accomplish tasks efficiently. Preserve the present configuration and state of your workspace in designated workspaces (e.g., Complete). This includes the whereabouts and preferences of palettes, toolbars, dialog boxes, and windows, in addition to all open images, magnifications, and screen positions.

Welcome Tab

The Welcome page is replete with educational materials, promotional offers, and critical details about your product. By utilizing this option, one can access the default workspace settings, initiate a fresh project, or access a file that was recently saved.

Manage Tab

Make use of the picture administration tools accessible via the Manage icon in the Complete workspace to assist with previewing, organizing, and streamlining the photo-editing process.

The administration components are as follows:

- **The navigation palette:** facilitates image organization and discovery. To enhance the efficiency of folder access on your computer, consider employing the search box, organizing photos by collection, categories, or ratings, or selecting the Collections or Computer tabs.

- **Two viewing options are available in the preview tab**: one is a large single-image view, and the other is a view featuring multiple thumbnails (expanded Organizer palette).

- **The information palette:** provides comprehensive details about the image that has been selected. The display presents the exposure settings of the photograph in a format resembling that of a camera. It also includes a segmented tab that allows users to input additional information, including ratings and annotations, as well as access a diverse array of EXIF or IPTC data.

- The organizer toolbar provides a multitude of choices and directives to oversee images. To modify the visibility of the instruments, press the button.

Edit Tab

To gain access to editing capabilities, navigate to the Edit tab. By the workspace, menus, tools, and palettes are accessible to generate and modify images.

Editing consists of the following choices:

1. **Menu bar:** Presents directives for carrying out operations. The Effects menu contains a variety of options for applying effects to your images.

2. **Toolbars:** Toolbars provide shortcuts to frequently executed commands.
3. **Palettes:** By displaying image data, palettes facilitate tool selection, choice modification, layer administration, color selection, and additional editing operations.
4. **Files** that are currently accessed will be exhibited in the image window. Additionally, a tabbed view and a window view are both options.
5. **Status Bar:** The status bar exhibits image dimensions, color depth, and cursor position. Unlike other toolbars, the status bar is immobile and located at the bottom of the window; it cannot be modified or relocated.

CUSTOMIZABLE TABS: ADJUST (FULL WORKSPACE)

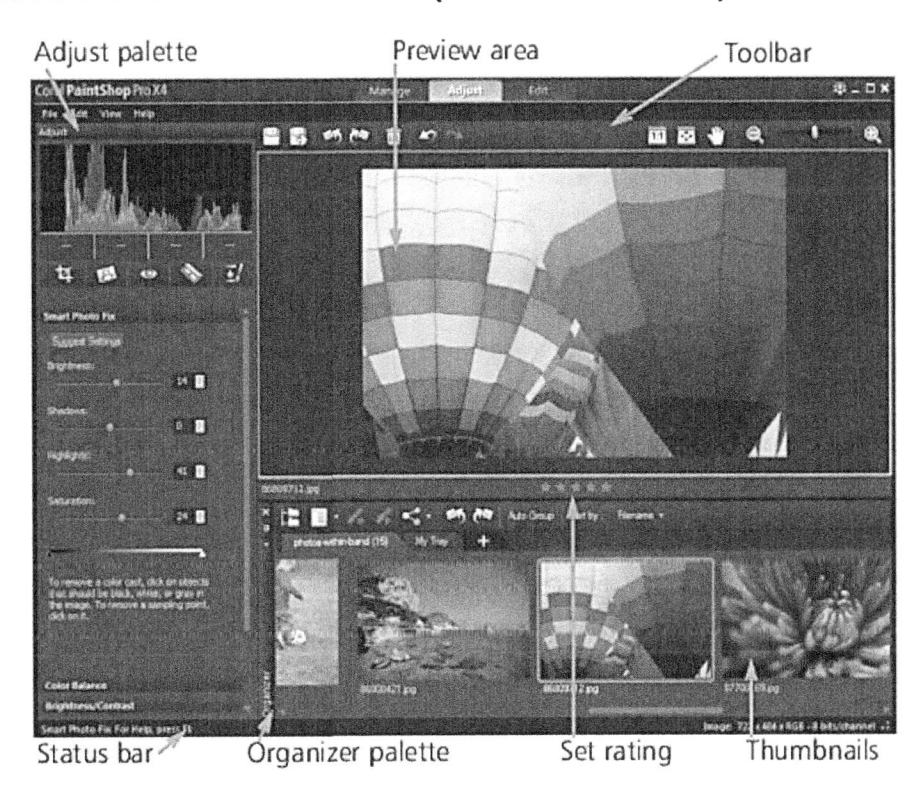

Adjust is the optimal application for speedy modifications. It provides an extensive selection of indispensable tools for enhancing and modifying images.

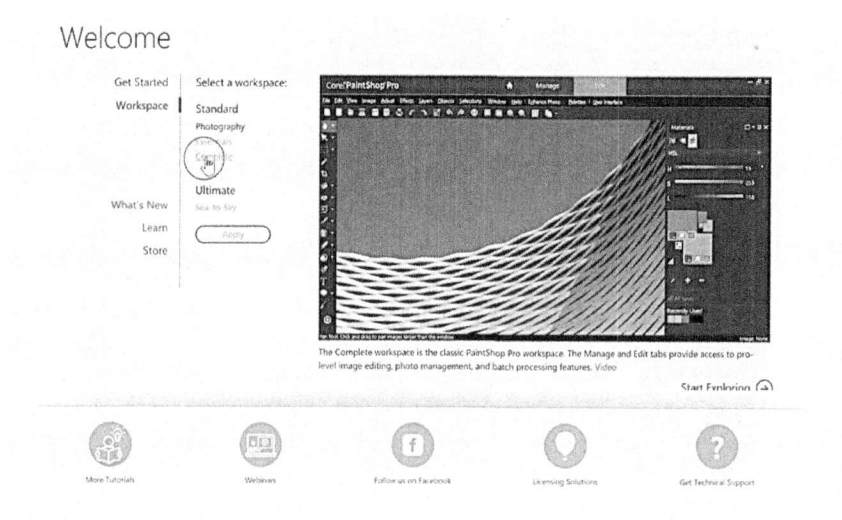

The Adjustment comprises the following elements:

- **Adjust palette:** Modify the palette to exhibit image adjustment controls and tools.
- **Preview section:** The image chosen from the Organizer palette is displayed in the Preview segment.
- **Toolbar:** The toolbar exhibits icons that facilitate frequent saving and viewing operations.
- **Organizer palette:** Select images to be displayed as thumbnails and gain access to a toolbar containing photo management commands and options.
- **Instant Effects Palette:** This palette contains a collection of preset effects that can be applied to a photograph. By clicking the icon, the instruments can be revealed or concealed.
- **Ratings:** Attain a rating for each image through the rating controls to facilitate the process of distinguishing your preferred ones.

Changing Between Tabs

With PaintShop Pro, you can effortlessly transition between pages to manage and edit your photos.

Here's how to transition between pages in your browser efficiently:

Select a category from the options displayed in the application's window:

- Welcome (Home icon).
- Task management across the entire workspace.
- Make adjustments in the complete workspace's options tab.
- Edit

Switching Between Various Workspaces

Users are provided with the choice to either create a personalized workspace or navigate between Photography, Essential, Complete, and specialty workspaces.

Switch Workspaces Efficiently

Choose one of the following options:

1. Select the desired workspace from the section labeled "Workspaces" on the Welcome page. The inventory of custom workspaces is not included in the Welcome pane.

2. By selecting File > Workspaces from the submenu, you can select your preferred workspace.

PHOTOGRAPHY WORKSPACE

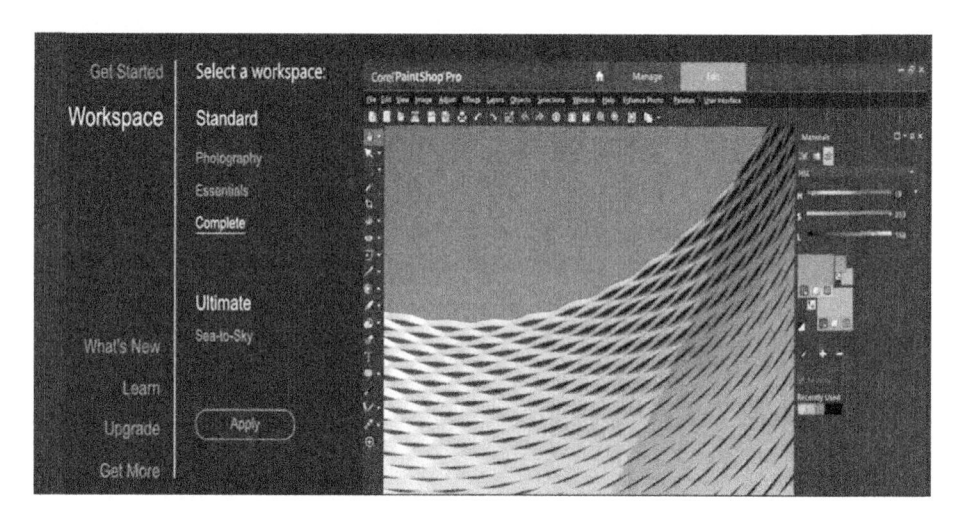

Split View, which is touch-responsive and designed to be intuitive for users, simplifies the editing process for novices in the Photography workspace. It is well-suited for integrating widely adopted improvements and modifications.

The tools found in the Photography workspace are also accessible in the Complete workspace, which features more streamlined iconography and components for full-screen use. For information regarding a particular instrument or configuration, please refer to the Help section and conduct a search using its name.

The Split View feature is absent from the Complete workspace. It is straightforward to enable or disable Split View by selecting the Split View icon from the Standard toolbar.

TOOLS TAILORED FOR YOUR PHOTOGRAPHY WORKSPACE

Certain instruments within the photography workspace necessitate only a single click, whereas others demand the modification of parameters. If applicable, the parameters for the selected instrument are displayed at the bottom of the window. Once the options have been modified, you have the option of selecting either the checkbox indication for Apply or the x sign for Cancel.

Adjustments can be made regularly, much like in other professional settings. Redo and Undo are buttons situated on the Tools toolbar's left side.

AI FEATURES IN PHOTOGRAPHY WORKSPACE

A plethora of artificial intelligence functionalities are readily obtainable within the photography sector. A brief amount of time is necessary to analyze these characteristics in depth. The processing performance can be affected by the image's dimensions and the utilized computer hardware. As soon as the AI completes its analysis of your image, a dynamic blue overlay will appear. To terminate processing temporarily, enter the Esc key.

For AI Style Transfer to function, the Instant Effects palette is required. If not already present, the Instant Effects palette is populated with the AI-Powered category when you select AI Style Transfer. Once a design thumbnail has been selected, it will be rendered in the preview. Doubling the click on a style miniature will result in its application to the image. It is not possible to compound styles; an existing style is replaced with a new style.

CHOOSE A COLOR SCHEME FOR YOUR WORKSPACE

There is a spectrum of tints found in workspaces, from dim to vibrant. Additionally, a backdrop color can be chosen for the image and preview windows.

When choosing the color of a workspace:

1. **Workspace Color** can be selected via the View menu.

2. Select a hue from the following list:

    - Gray-Black (standard)
    - Gray Medium
    - Gray Light

Bear in mind that you must modify the color by selecting **User Interface > Workspace Color**.

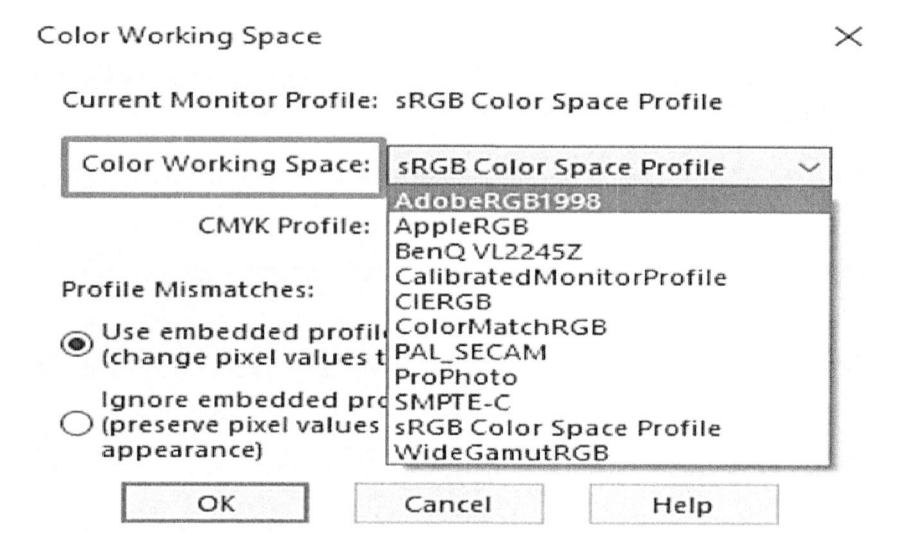

How to Adjust the Color of Your Background

1. To modify the background color, select **View > Background Color**.

2. To modify the color of the background, select User Interface > Background Color.

USING PALETTES

PaintShop Pro provides a variety of palettes for organizing data and image manipulation instructions. Certain palettes will appear immediately upon tool activation, whereas others will only manifest upon the tool's opening. By selecting View Palettes, it is possible to activate and deactivate a palette with ease. Specific palettes can solely be accessed through specific tabs.

Palettes, which can additionally encompass command icons and controllers, are utilized to exhibit data. Similar to toolbars, palettes can be conveniently moved from their initial docked state.

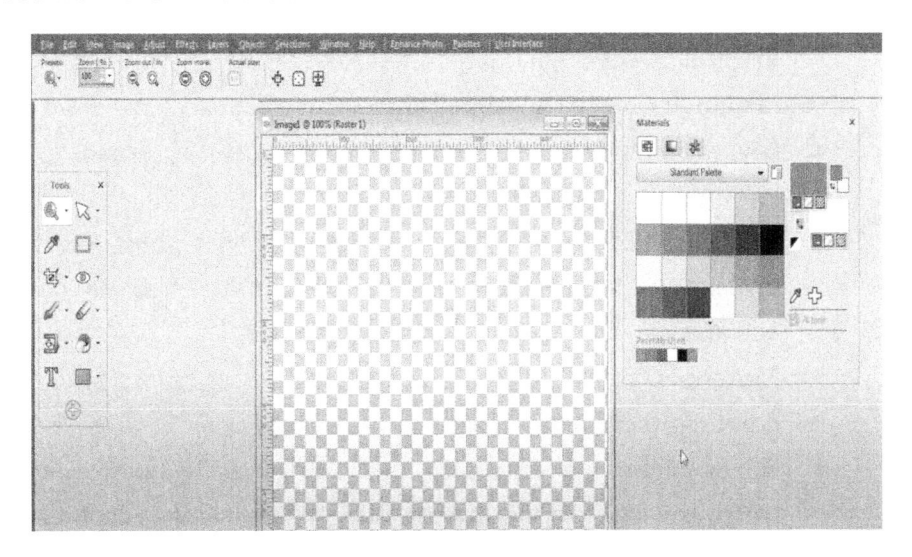

The description of the palette is as follows:

- **Brush Variance:** Additionally customizable brush parameters are available when utilizing a paintbrush or any other raster painting tool. This palette is immensely beneficial when manipulating a four-dimensional mouse or a pressure-sensitive tablet. To illustrate, the intensity of a brushstroke can be modified by manipulating the stylus pressure. Certain alternatives are also operable via a mouse.
- **Histogram:** Displays a graphical representation that depicts the distribution of the grayscale, saturation, luminance, and red, green, and blue values of an image, in addition to these values. An essential consideration in determining the necessary corrections is the analysis of detail distribution across the highlights, midtones, and shadows.
- **History:** This feature furnishes a log of the operations performed on the present image, grants the capability to reverse or revert recent or

previous actions, and facilitates the rapid execution of a Quick script on other active images.

- **Info Palette:** The Info palette, situated on the Manage menu, presents details about the image that has been selected. A camera-style interface presents the photo's settings, while a segmented area facilitates the viewing and modification of information including location details, ratings, tags, EXIF and IPTC data, and ratings.
- **Instant Effects:** Facilitates effortless image modification by offering instant access to thumbnails of preset effects.
- **Layers:** Utilize the Layers feature to observe, organize, and delete parameters for image layers.
- **Learning Center:** Offers comprehensive guidance, tools, and procedures to facilitate the efficient and effective completion of activities.
- **Materials:** From the materials menu, select colors and materials for painting, sketching, filling, and retouching.
- **Mixer:** Blend pigments with the Oil Brush and Palette Knife tools using the Mixer tool to generate realistic oil paint strokes on Art Media layers.
- **Overview:** Presenting a thumbnail of the active image, enabling the user to adjust the magnification level, and providing information about the image.
- **Organizer:** Select, modify, email, or print photographs using the organizer. It compiles and exhibits photographs from numerous folders. By renaming, deleting, and creating containers within the palette, one can tailor them to a particular workflow.
- **Script Output:** An abridged version of the actions and outcomes that transpire after the execution of the script.
- **Tool Options:** Exhibiting the configurations and management elements of the active tool.

Show a Palette

1. Select **View > Palettes**, followed by the palette's name. A checkbox is used to indicate which palettes are active and visible at the moment.

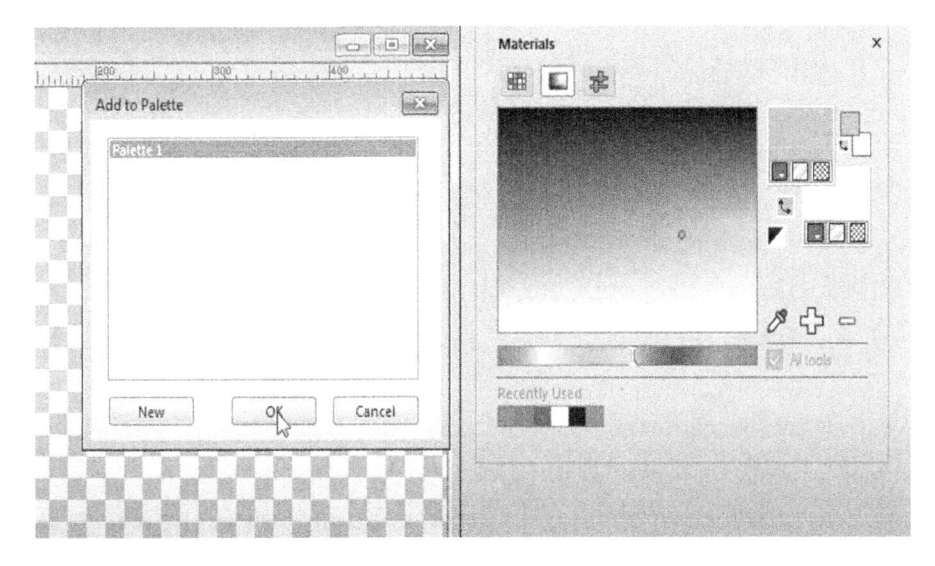

2. It should be noted that the ability to reveal or hide a floating palette can be achieved by tapping F2.

Resizing a Palette

1. From the Edit pane, modify the dimensions of a palette by dragging one of its corners or edges.

2. To ensure effortless resizing of a docked palette, remember to select the **Minimize palette icon** situated in the title bar.

WORKING WITH THE VARIOUS TOOLBARS

The work area is furnished with toolbars that include practical icons for executing routine activities. A tooltip is exhibited when the user hovers over a button, revealing its name, whereas the status bar furnishes supplementary details about the command. On the Edit menu, the Learning Center provides instructions on how to optimize the utility.

The following toolbars are predominantly located on the Edit tab:

- **Effects:** Instructions for applying effects to your photographs are provided.
- **Photos:** Instructions are given regarding the process of enhancing images.
- **Script:** The script provides direction for the creation and execution of scripts.
- **Standard:** Positioned atop the interface, the standard option offers commonly used file-management functionalities such as the ability to save photos, undo commands, and copy and paste objects.
- **Tools:** An assortment of tools for image modification tasks, including painting, drawing, cropping, and text entry, are located in this section of the window.
- **Status:** Located at the bottom of the box, this section typically presents information about the instrument that is presently selected.
- **Web:** Guidelines for generating and conserving photographs for the Internet are presented.

How can the Visibility of a Toolbar be Toggled?

By selecting **View > Toolbars**, you can locate the toolbar that you wish to conceal or display. In the menu, the toolbar is visible when a checkbox appears next to its name. To access the toolbars from the Edit pane, select the desired toolbar by right-clicking on any of them, selecting **Toolbars**, and then entering its name. To conceal the toolbar, navigate to the title bar and select the **Close button**.

Use the Tools at your Disposal

These instruments possess a wide range of applications in the fields of image manipulation and artistic endeavors. The tooltips exhibit the names and shortcut keys of the tools that are being hovered over. Additionally, utilization suggestions are presented in the status bar.

Access a diverse selection of sophisticated tools for creating and editing images by selecting the Edit tab. The Tools toolbar contains a variety of applications, including the Text, Crop, and Move tools. The majority of tools are commonly coupled with other instruments that accomplish similar tasks. A set of tools is denoted by a miniature flyout arrow situated to the right of the present tool.

The type of layer that is being edited can restrict the accessibility of specific tools. The Pen tool functions exclusively on vector-containing layers, whereas the Paint Brush and Clone Brush tools operate exclusively on raster layers.

A concise description of each utility located in the Tools toolbar on the Edit pane follows:

- **Pan:** The image window's display can be customized to display a particular region of the image by utilizing the pan function.
- **Zoom:** Modifies the perspective with a left or right click. A region to be magnified can be selected through the use of dragging.

- **Pick:** Working with raster layers allows for effortless rotation, reshaping, and movement. Conversely, vector objects can be selected and modified as required.
- **Move:** This function relocates a raster or vector layer on the canvas.
- **Automated Selection:** When you enclose an area in a selection rectangle, the software detects its boundaries automatically.
- **Smart Selection Brush:** Presenting the Smart Selection Brush, which selects the perimeters of a given region automatically as you move the brush across a sample area.
- **Selection:** Choose a geometric shape such as a triangle, ellipse, or rectangle when making a selection.

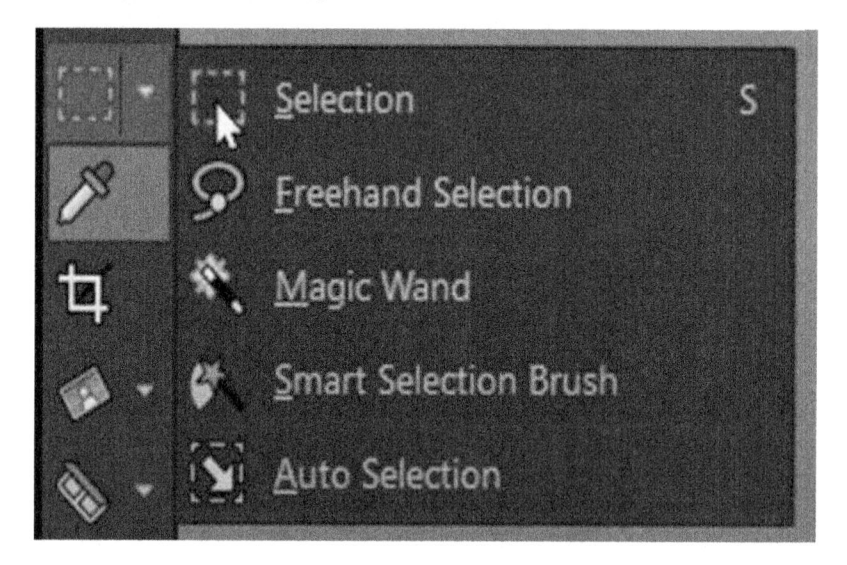

- **Freehand Selection:** The process of producing an assortment in an atypical form.
- **Magic wand:** The Magic Wand tool is utilized to select pixels that fall within a predetermined tolerance threshold.
- **Dropper:** The background/fill color can be chosen via right-clicking, while the foreground/stroke color can be selected by selecting.
- **Crop:** To achieve a neat appearance, it is critical to eliminate or trim any extraneous margins. A variety of options for enhancing images can be accessed via the crop toolbar.

- **Straighten:** To appropriately align a distorted image, rotate it.
- **Perspective Correction:** Correction of perspective involves the rectification of the slanted appearance of objects or structures.
- **Red Eye:** Effectively resolves red-eye issues in photographs
- **Makeover:** Optimise your photographs with the assistance of five distinct aesthetic modification settings: ThinifyTM, Blemish Fixer, Toothbrush, Eye Drop, and Suntan.
- **Clone:** The act of painting over a clone serves to obscure any imperfections or objects present in the image.
- **Smart Clone:** The replicating tool's content awareness enables seamless integration of a chosen source into a new background.
- **Scratch Remover:** Eliminates blemishes and other linear flaws from digital photographs captured by scanning software.
- **Object Removal:** Masks undesirable regions in a shot using a neighboring texture within the same image.
- **Paint Brush:** This tool allows for the addition of colors, textures, or gradients to an image.
- **Airbrushes:** Spray cans or airbrushes are utilized to apply paint to replicate the appearance of airbrush painting.
- **Brightness Adjustment:** By employing the right mouse button while dragging, specific segments will undergo a modification in brightness. The magnitude of this impact surpasses that of the effects generated by the Dodge and Burn tools.
- **Dodge:** Permits you to right-click and adjust the luminance of specific areas in an image.
- **Burn:** Through right-clicking, you can modify the luminosity or darkness of specified areas in an image.
- **Smudge:** The right mouse button provides the user with the choice to either press pixels without acquiring new colors or smear pixels by accumulating new colors while dragging.
- **Push:** Either smears pixels by selecting additional colors during right-clicked mouse drag, or propels pixels by forgoing color selection during drag.

- **Soften:** To apply a softening effect to an image, tap and hold the right mouse button while dragging to obscure or intensify the pixels.
- **Sharpen:** By employing the right mouse button while dragging, pixels can be adjusted to be either sharper or softer.
- **Emboss:** Creates the appearance of emboss by tracing edges while suppressing color.
- **Hue Adjustment:** To modify the hue values of individual pixels, employ the right mouse button and drag the selection vertically.
- **Change target:** Recolor individual pixels while preserving their detail.
- **Color replacer:** The background/fill color is substituted for the foreground/stroke color when the user clicks and drags. By right-clicking and dragging, the background/fill color is applied in place of the foreground/stroke color.
- **Eraser function:** Eliminates transparent pixels from the raster layer
- **Flood Fill:** With a right-click or a click, pixels of the same tolerance level will be filled with the current foreground/stroke material or the current background/fill material using Flood Fill.
- **Gradient Fill:** Adds interactive gradient fills to images to enhance them.
- **Picture Tube:** Picture tubes and other imaginative components that correspond to a particular theme can be integrated into an image.
- **Text:** Include text within the image.
- **Frame Tool:** The Frame Tool produces a frame suitable for inserting images.
- **Preset Shape:** Integrate pre-established shapes, such as arrows, callouts, and starbursts, into your image.
- **Rectangle:** Constructs a rectangle or square shape.
- **Ellipse:** Produces an ellipse or a circle.
- **Symmetrical shape:** Produces celestial or symmetrical objects.
- **Pen:** Segments of Bézier curves, freehand curves, and connected or disconnected lines can be generated with the pen.

ADJUST YOUR PALETTES AND TOOLBARS

Particularly from the Edit tab, you can modify the toolbars and palettes by anchoring, floating, resizing, and rearranging them to tailor your workspace. Palettes and toolbars can merge automatically when docking is enabled. Without synchronization, toolbars and palettes can be positioned autonomously on the display.

You are provided with the choice to either display the toolbars and palettes or conceal them when they are not required.

HOW TO SET UP YOUR PREFERRED DOCKING METHOD

Follow the following steps:

1. Choose **View > Options for Docking**.
2. Select the palettes that you wish to dock by entering them into the group box provided. Even if a palette is configured for docking, it can be effortlessly relocated to a different location by dragging it while holding down the Ctrl key.

How to Dock a Toolbar or Palette

Align the title bar of the toolbar or palette with the edge of the window. The palette or toolbar can lock into position. To suspend toolbars and palettes, double-click their title bars.

How to Float a Toolbar or Palette and Achieve it

1. Choose one of the alternatives provided:
   - Position the pointer over the toolbar's handle. The cursor transforms into an icon of a four-sided mobile.
   - Position the cursor within the palette's title bar.
2. By dragging, the toolbar or palette can be removed from the window's edge.

The dimensions and positioning of the handle are determined by the toolbar's orientation and size. Additionally, you can double-click the toolbar's handle.

How to Move a Palette or a Toolbar within an Application

When relocating a palette or toolbar:

- Alter the placement of the title bar associated with the Edit tab.

To modify the size of a palette or toolbar:

- Modify the dimensions of the interface or palette by manipulating a corner or side.

Ensure the visibility of all palettes and toolbars.

- Utilize Ctrl + Shift + T.

Raise a Toolbar or Palette

Select the **Auto Hide pushpin icon** from the toolbar or palette's title bar. Notwithstanding the Auto Hide pushpin being positioned downward, the toolbar or pallet retains complete visibility. If the Auto Hide pushpin is positioned to the left, the toolbar or palette will roll up when the user moves the cursor away.

By carrying out an operation that preserves the focus of the toolbar or palette, it will be possible to observe the toolbar or palette even after the cursor has been moved. The toolbar or pallet will automatically retract itself upon performing another action or clicking elsewhere.

Depending on its state when the Auto Hide feature is enabled, the palette or toolbar will collapse differently when you click away: If it is attached, a tab containing the name will appear; if it is floating, only the title bar will be visible.

Re-pressing the **Auto Hide button** will stop the rolling of the palette. Verify that the cursor is still positioned above the tab to reload the palette.

WORKING WITH DIALOG BOXES

Windows dialog boxes appear upon selecting particular PaintShop Pro commands. Selecting and viewing the command options is possible. Dialog boxes will reappear in the precise location where they were previously closed on the screen.

Two distinct designs of dialog boxes are at one's disposal. Filters such as Depth of Field, Smart Photo Fix, Graduated Filter, Red Eye Removal, Retro Lab, Selective Focus, and Vignette are accessible via the Adjust and Effect menu. A wider layout is employed to facilitate navigation when navigating interactive settings.

Many dialog panels possess the following characteristics in common:

- **Presets** exhibit pre-established configurations, also known as templates, which can be utilized to modify images efficiently. Utilizing the Before and After panels, observe the impact of the dialog box settings on your image.
- The controls for Zoom and Pan enable the modification of the present viewing area.
- One can utilize the Reset to Default icon to restore the dialog box to its initial configuration.
- Color boxes enable the selection of colors for a given command option.
- By selecting the randomize parameters icon, one can observe a preview of various configurations.
- Utilize the edit controls to select or enter numeric values.

Using the Preview Areas Efficiently

Adjusting selections, applying effects, or augmenting image features are the most common uses for dialog boxes. Before and After panes display the image after the modifications have been made. The Show/Hide Previews button provides the capability to either exhibit or conceal the Before and After panels within specific dialog boxes.

Whether the Before and After apertures are visible or concealed depends on the circumstances.

Verify that the Preview on the Image option is selected in the dialog box's upper-right corner so that you can continue to observe the effect of the current settings on the image even when the Before and After panes are hidden. By selecting the icon adjacent to the preview, one can conceal the Before and After windows.

GUIDANCE FOR ZOOMING IN AND OUT OF THE PICTURE PREVIEW

Make modifications to the Zoom parameter. Expanding the dialog box will increase the available space in the Before and After panes.

How to Pan a Preview Image

The stages are as follows:

1. The cursor should be positioned in the After pane. A hand is utilized in its place as the cursor.

2. Replace the image.

3. Maintain the desired area of the image in the center of the selection rectangle by holding down the Pan Button.

Proof Changes in the Main Image Window

Select the Preview on the Image checkbox located beneath the Edit tab. Modifications made in a dialog pane will be reflected automatically in the primary image window.

How to Professionally Edit the Numeric Values

Select a task from the following list:

- Enter the new value after selecting **Backspace or Delete** from the control menu.
- To modify the value, simply press the corresponding up or down arrow.
- Make an estimation of a value selection using the slider.
- To navigate through the available settings, manipulate the slider.
- Inputting a value that deviates from the permissible range will result in the control turning red. To input a new value, merely highlight the number with two clicks.

How to Select a Color from your Dialog Box

Choose an assignment from the provided options:

- To choose a color, merely click the color box and then select the desired hue from the resulting color dialog box.
- Using the recent color dialog box, select a hue by right-clicking the color box.

Modify Settings in a Dialog Box at Random.

Proceed with the following steps:

- Select the icon labeled "Randomize parameters" from the Edit pane.

- By repeatedly selecting the Randomize parameters icon until the intended result is obtained, one can conduct experiments with various values.

HOW TO VIEW YOUR IMAGES

To view images in tabbed mode, an additional tab will appear at the top of the image window. The image in the window that appears when you select a tab is updated to reflect the current image. The ability to dismiss, reposition, and resize windows allows for continuous image viewing. To manipulate the image's magnification, it can be viewed in multiple image windows or tabs.

You can easily arrange the image panes to display multiple photographs side by side or layered. You can either resize the image window to accommodate the image or pan to view various portions of the image if it is larger than the image window. The Overview palette presents a thumbnail representation of the complete image.

The filename and the percentage of magnification are displayed in the title bar located at the top of the image window. The modifications made to the image have not been stored, as the asterisk following the filename indicates. In addition to the image's identity, a copyright indicator will be presented when the image includes a watermark.

Turn the Tabbed Image Window Option on or Off

The stages are as follows:

1. Select **Window > Tabbed Documents** from the menu labeled Edit.

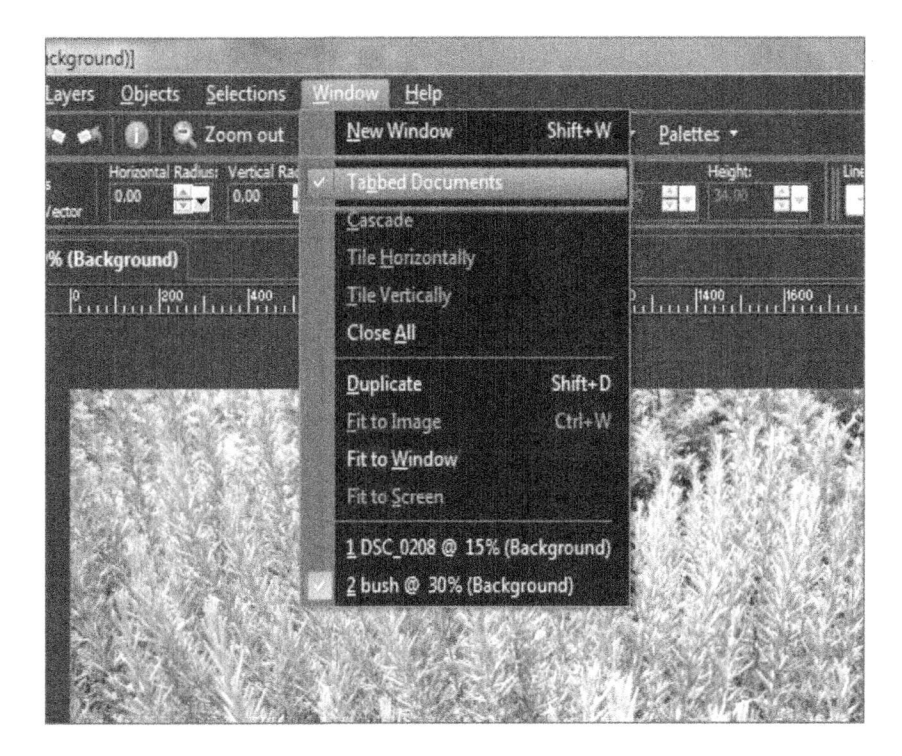

2. To access an alternative image, one need only choose the corresponding tab. If the current view does not display an image pane, you can navigate to the left or right using the arrows located in the upper-right quadrant of the image window.

3. To dismiss the image in tabbed format, click the dismiss icon.

Optimize the Size of the Image Window

Select a task from the following list:

- Selecting the **Minimize icon** will cause the image window to be reduced to the title bar only.

- By selecting the **Maximize icon**, the image window will enlarge to encompass the entire screen.

Close the Image Window

Follow the steps below:

- After selecting File, select **Close**. Save your modifications if you have altered an image. The Close icon is located in the title bar.

- Select **Window > Close All** to terminate all currently active windows.

How can I Duplicate the image Currently on the Screen?

- Navigate to **Window > Duplicate**. It seems that the existing image is a duplicate. You can modify a copy of the original image as you see fit when working with it.

- By holding down **Shift + D**, the currently selected image is duplicated.

Arranging Multiple Windows on Your Screen

Please select one of the following alternatives:

- To enable cascading windows, select the **Windows > Cascade** option. In a diagonal arrangement, the windows progress from the upper left corner to the lower right corner.

- To exhibit windows in a vertical orientation, navigate to **Windows > Tile Vertically**. Windows are capable of being adjusted to suit precisely within the window.

- To arrange windows horizontally, select **Window > Tile Horizontally**. It is possible to adjust Windows to suit precisely within the screen.

To Examine a Different Section of the Image

Carry out the following measures:

- Select the Pan tool from the Tools interface, and subsequently drag the image into the window, to pan the image. While dragging the image, remember to click and hold the Spacebar if another tool is selected.

- Modify horizontal or vertical vision adjustments by correspondingly repositioning the scroll bar.

- After displaying the Overview interface by selecting F9 on the keyboard, navigate to the Preview tab, position the cursor within the panning rectangle, and initiate a dragging motion. Additionally, the Zoom level can be modified via the Preview menu located in the Overview palette.

Adjust the Image to fit within the Image Window

Carry out the following actions:

- To resize the window to the image, select **Window > Fit** Image.

- To adjust the dimensions of the image to suit the window, select **Window** followed by **Fit to Window.**

- To adjust the window and image to suit the screen, choose **Window > Fit to Screen**.

USING KEYBOARD SHORTCUTS FOR ENHANCED EFFICIENCY

To efficiently navigate the menu, select tools, display palettes, manipulate nodes on vector objects, and execute Organizer commands in PaintShop Pro , utilize the shortcut keys. A comprehensive list of auxiliary keys is provided for every menu command, including those utilized to access palettes. When you hover over a tool, the shorthand commands associated with that tool will be displayed.

HOW TO ACCESS A DETAILED LIST OF ALL AVAILABLE CONTEXT MENUS

Follow the following steps:

1. Select **Customize** from the menu labeled View.
2. Navigate to the **Menu tab**.
3. Select a value from the drop-down menu contextual menu.

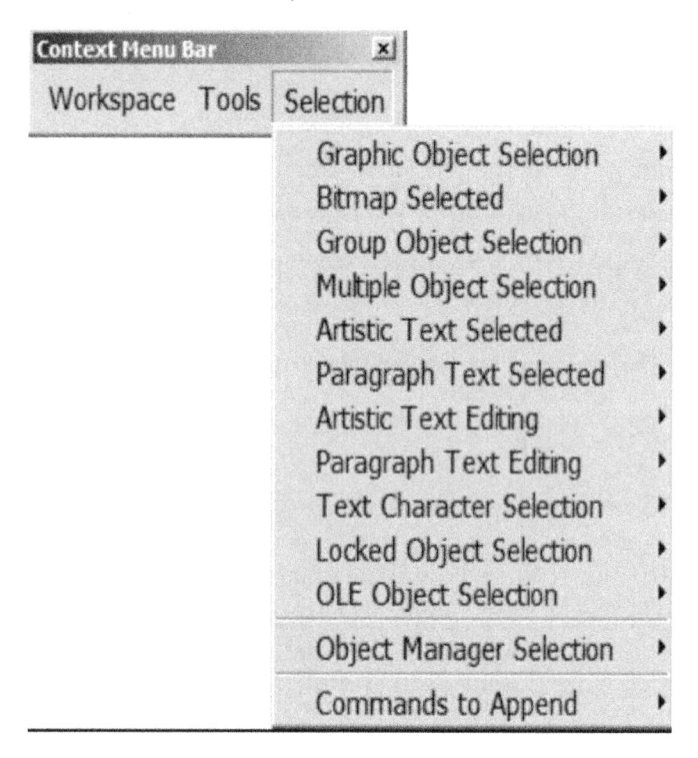

4. The drop-down menu comprises the names of every item available in the context menu. Select it to bring up a context-specific menu.

Guidelines for Utilizing a Context-Accessible Menu

Follow the following steps:

1. A toolbar, an image, a location within a palette, a layer within the Layers palette, or a thumbnail in the Organizer can be accessed via right-clicking.
2. Continue by selecting a command.

GRID

By default, the rulers are presented on the Edit pane. Users are provided with the choice to modify the rulers' color, exhibit them in units of pixels, inches, or centimeters, or obfuscate them entirely.

What are Grids?

The overlay on your image consists of a grid composed of both vertical and horizontal lines. Positioning image components is possible via grid lines. Grids can be hidden or displayed, and their spacing and appearance can be modified. Grids are rendered in all active image windows.

What are Guides?

You can position guides on your image in either a horizontal or vertical orientation. When rulers are displayed, you can precisely crop images, move components, make selections, and add text and brushstrokes by utilizing the guidelines on your image. Guides are customizable, as opposed to grids which produce horizontal and vertical lines at predetermined intervals.

Adjusting the Snapping Feature

The utilization of snapping allows for the accurate alignment of brushstrokes and image elements with the closest grid or guide. Determining the minimum distance an element must be from a grid line or guide to snap to it is dependent on the snap influence. A snap is executed when the center point of an object coincides with a grid or guide.

SETTING RULER PROPERTIES

The stages are as follows:

- To gain access to the **General Program Preferences**, select **File > Preferences**.
- Choose the **Units** option from the selection.

- Input a selected option from the Display Units navigation menu into the Rulers field.

- To select the hue of the ruler, choose one of the following alternatives:
    - **Toolbar colors:** Black hash marks and numerals contrast with a palette of hues, which is a prevalent motif in toolbars and palettes.
    - **Black on white:** A design that showcases black punctuation marks and numerals set against a backdrop of white.

- Click the OK button.

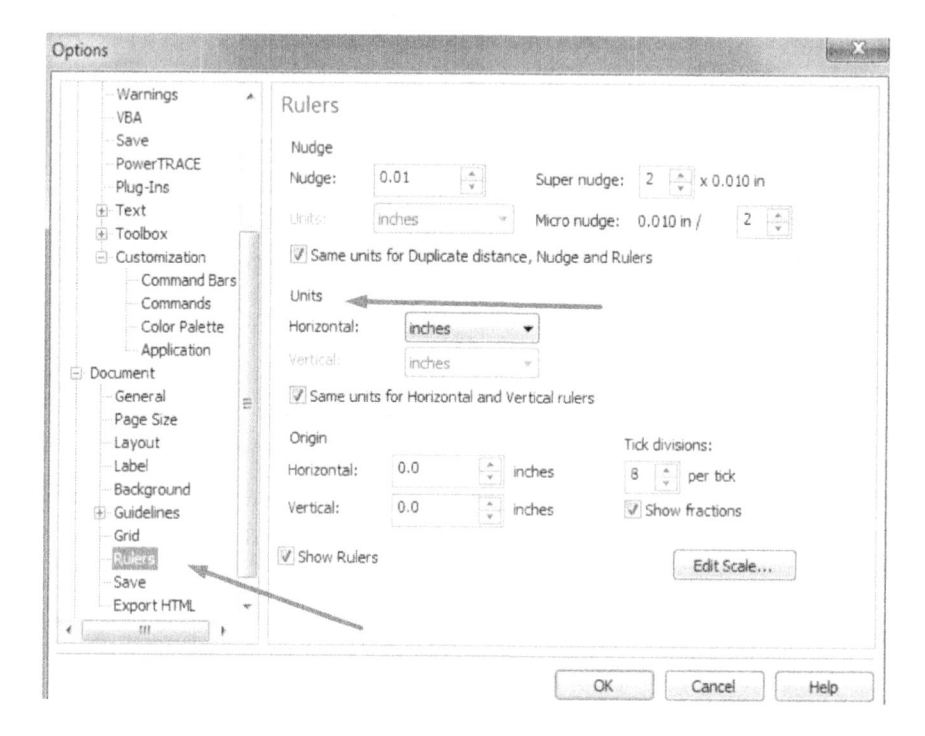

Exploring Grid Properties and how to Customize them

Follow the following steps:

- Modify the grid, guide, and snap properties by navigating to the View menu.

- Ensure that the Grid tab is selected. The default configurations for the grid are presented in the Default settings group box. In the group box labeled "Current image settings," the grid configurations for the current image are exhibited.
- To achieve accurate modifications, simply enter the desired value into the horizontal grid control or manually transcribe it from the upper portion of the image.
- To achieve exact modifications, simply enter a value into the Vertical grid control or type the desired spacing from the image's left side.
- Utilize the Units drop-down menu to designate a unit of measurement.
- Click the OK button.

You are presented with the chance to elevate it to a higher degree:

- Select a hue from the available color palette by selecting it via the Color box.
- Modify the level of snap influence by inputting a value into the Snap Influence Control.

SET UP A VERTICAL OR HORIZONTAL GUIDE

The stages are as follows:

1. Navigate to **View > Rulers** to enable the rulers.

2. Select Guides via the menu labeled View.

3. Select one of the options listed below:

    - Dragging a guide while clicking the upper ruler will establish a horizontal guide.

    - To establish a vertical guide, click and drag a guide on the left ruler. As you drag, the location of the aid is displayed in the Status bar (in pixels).

4. To obtain further positioning options, operate the ruler by double-clicking a guide handle. A dialog box containing guide properties for experts appears.

5. Enter or input a value into the Guide position control.

6. Click the OK button.

Guidelines for Adjusting the Color of a Guide

Follow the following steps:

1. Double-click a ruler's guide handle.
2. By selecting the Color option on the Guides pane, one can select a color from the color palette.
3. Click the OK button.

ADDING IMAGES TO COREL PAINTSHOP PRO

Proceed to import the captured images into PaintShop Pro after their transfer to the computer via the camera's software or Windows. Images can be imported by navigating through folders. The folders' images are automatically classified in a database. It streamlines the procedure of locating, modifying, and updating image data.

The stages are as follows:

1. In the Navigation panel, select the Collections tab and then navigate to Browse More Folders.

2. Select the desired folder via the Browse For Folder menu.

3. Click the OK button.

The folder has been appended to the list of folders, and every image has been cataloged in the application database. The Navigation palette will become visible when the **Show/Hide Navigation button** on the Organizer palette is selected.

Establishing Connections with Multiple Image Scanners

A picture-scanning application can be selected from within the scanning program. PaintShop Pro is compatible with an extensive range of TWAIN, WIA, and USB scanners.

SAVING IMAGES

When saving an image, be mindful of the file format and avoid overwriting any originals that you can require in the future.

PaintShop Pro supports layers, alpha channels, and an assortment of image-creation tools via the PspImage file format. You can edit and save your images in PspImage format. The files can be saved in common file formats. You can utilize the Save for Office command to convert your images for utilization in an alternative program, such as an email client, web page design application, or page layout program.

The following are frequent file formats:

- **JPEG:** A prevalent digital image file format, JPEG is well-suited for transmission via email and the web. To reduce file size, lossy compression is implemented; however, it results in a progressive deterioration of image quality with each save. Selecting a high-quality alternative is critical when contemplating image modification. This file format is compatible with EXIF and IPTC data, which contain details such as the date the image was captured.

- **TIFF:** TIFF is an extensively utilized file format that facilitates the printing and transfer of photographs across various software applications. By employing lossless compression, this particular file format is maintained. While the larger file size does not undermine the image's quality during the saving process, it cannot be optimal for online or email sharing. For printing purposes, the TIFF format is compatible with EXIF and IPTC data and can preserve information in CMYK color mode.

- **PNG:** PNG is a prevalent image file format utilized on the Internet. Non-lossy compression is utilized to decrease the file size, thereby guaranteeing the accurate retention of image data.

- **RAW:** RAW file formats are frequently employed by professionals in the photography industry. The greatest flexibility in image processing is provided by RAW camera formats, which deliver uncompressed, raw image data. A camera capable of capturing images in RAW format and software capable of reading and editing the files, such as PaintShop Pro, is essential.

A PspImage file can be saved in either an uncompressed or compressed state. Two lossless compression techniques are utilized by PaintShop Pro to reduce file size without sacrificing image quality. Uncompressed files require a more substantial amount of disk space.

- Run-length encoding (RLE), one of the compression methods utilized in PaintShop Pro, can decrease the dimensions of multilayer images to approximately 75% of their initial dimensions. Aspects of an image that contain consistent coloration lend themselves well to this method.

- Although LZ77 compression requires more time than RLE compression, it reduces the size of the majority of images more significantly. This method is extraordinarily effective due to the incredibly realistic images it generates.

When storing a new image in PaintShop Pro, the location, file type, and name can be specified. An asterisk or modifier will be displayed in the picture title bar while an image is being edited or saved. Once the work has been saved, this identifier is eliminated.

Establish automatic file saves to safeguard your work in the event of an unexpected computer termination. To preserve a version of a file, an image can be duplicated and saved. Using this function to apply effects to an image while preserving the original file can be extremely beneficial.

Always utilize the Auto-Preserve Original option to prevent the overwriting of original photographs. This function is generally enabled.

HOW TO PROPERLY SAVE A NEW IMAGE

Proceed by following these steps:

1. Navigate to **File > Save**.
2. Select the desired folder for file storage from the drop-down menu.

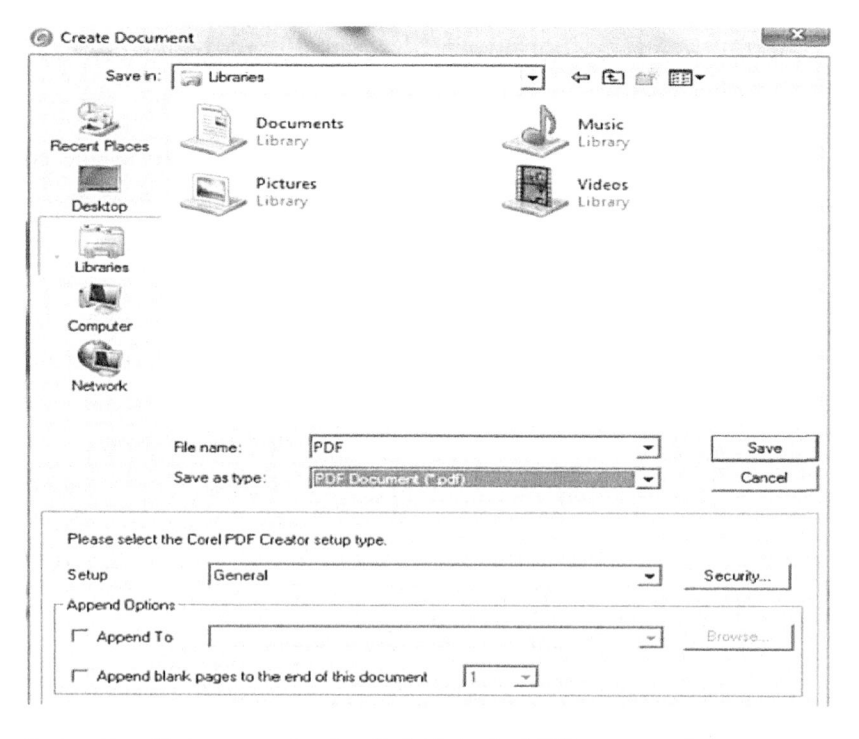

3. Enter the file's name in the field labeled "**File name**."

4. Choose a file format from the drop-down menu labeled Save as type. The most frequently utilized formats are presented initially. To modify the default settings for the file format, select the desired parameters from the Options menu, such as color profile or compression.

5. Select the Save button. To prevent the need to overwrite your current file, contemplate conserving your work by selecting the Save As option located on the Standard interface.

Utilize the Compression toggle to modify the default settings for JPEG images before storing them for the first time during an editing session. To gain entry to the General Program Preferences, select File followed by Preferences. To save in the format of the most recently accessed file, select Display and Caching from the list on the left. In the Presentation group section of the File Save-As Dialog, select the checkbox labeled Reuse Last Type.

CHAPTER THREE

COREL RAW IMAGES

RAW IMAGE IN PAINTSHOP PRO

RAW format is an option that is available on an overwhelming majority of digital single-lens reflex cameras. In comparison to the JPEG format, the RAW mode exhibits an enhanced capacity to capture a substantial quantity of image data. RAW image data is comparable to an adversarial negative in that it is uncompressed and unaltered, allowing for unrestricted printing. The Camera RAW Lab in PaintShop Pro functions as a virtual darkroom, providing users with the ability to manipulate and refine RAW files.

After RAW processing, modifications can be implemented by exporting the image to a PNG, JPEG, or GIF file. Conversely, one can opt to maintain the RAW file in a read-only condition. XMP files can also be periodically updated and read.

Camera RAW Lab is capable of decoding RAW files in formats that are typical RAW files. These formats are compatible with RAW file formats produced by the industry's foremost camera manufacturers. A list that is deemed current can be found in the Corel Knowledge Base.

PUT CAMERA RAW LAB TO USE

A diverse range of processing configurations can be preserved within the Camera RAW Lab, facilitating the creation of RAW images. After making modifications to a RAW image, the Edit pane provides the capability to export the image to an alternative file format, including JPEG, GIF, or PNG. Alternatively, the image can be preserved as a read-only RAW file.

Launch the Camera RAW Lab

Select one of the options that follow from the provided list:

1. After selecting a RAW image file, navigate to File > Open in the Manage menu. Following that, select the **Open icon**.

2. From the context menu that appears when you right-click on one or more thumbnails located under the Manage pane, select **Edit RAW**.

3. To access the picture window, double-click or drag a RAW image thumbnail from the Organizer palette. An alternative option is to select the **Edit tab**.

Adjust RAW Images Settings

Follow the following steps:

1. Navigate to the Camera RAW Lab dialog window and select one of the following options based on your personal preferences:

    - To rapidly modify the entirety of the image, one can employ the sliders designated for shadow, saturation, and brightness.

    - Modify the color within the White Balance section by selecting a pre-established illumination option from the Scenario drop-list or by utilizing the Eyedropper tool to adjust the white point by tapping the preview area. There are both of these options available. In addition, color adjustments and fine-tuning are possible via the Tint and Temperature sliders.

    - Select an item from the drop-down menu, and subsequently hover your mouse over it in the specified region to recover the highlight. The highlight recovery process is highly advantageous for overexposed images due to its capability of aiding in the restoration of detail in regions that have been excessively illuminated.

    - Implementing the Threshold slider within the "Minimize Noise" section represents the most effective method for reducing digital noise. The modifications that have been applied to the image can be viewed in the Preview pane. To preserve the photo settings for future reference, please ensure that the checkbox at the bottom of the page is checked.

2. Using the toggle, choose one of the following options:

    - All right, this exits the Camera RAW Lab and permanently modifies the settings.
    - Cancel - Clicking the Cancel icon terminates the Camera RAW Lab without affecting the configuration of the captured image.

3. In the thumbnail row, click the "**Add more photos**" icon to submit additional images to the Camera RAW Lab. To address lens-related complications, select the Lens pane (maximum of 30 images). The parameters of RAW-formatted images are stored in a database. If modifications are executed using Corel PaintShop Pro, the database will possess the capability to monitor any alterations implemented to the file name or location.

Adjust Several RAW Images

One of the most common responsibilities of photographers, particularly those who utilize DSLR cameras, is the organization and editing of a substantial quantity of images. It is conceivable that one might encounter a situation in which they are downloading a collection of images that require comparable processing power and were captured in entirely identical settings. Once the modifications to a single image have been duplicated in the Camera RAW Lab, PaintShop Pro can be utilized to efficiently implement the identical adjustments to a collection of photographs.

HOW TO CONVERT IMAGES TAKEN IN RAW FORMAT TO ANOTHER FORMAT

It is critical to mention that the RAW file format operates in read-only mode, and its parameters are contained within a distinct preamble. It is possible to modify these configurations through the Camera RAW Lab. To utilize the editing tools accessible through the Edit pane, it is necessary to convert the RAW file to a different file format, including JPEG, TIFF, or the original format. Depicting PSP. To expedite the conversion process, utilize Convert RAW

How to Convert a RAW Picture to a Different File Type?

Steps to take:

1. Select a thumbnail from the Organizer interface, or multiple thumbnails, from the RAW file.
2. Once a thumbnail has been chosen from the menu, proceed by selecting the Convert RAW button.
3. Under the "Type" drop-down menu in the Batch Process dialog box, choose a file format. After selecting the Options option, proceed to modify the necessary settings to update the conversion's default parameters.
4. Select the desired folder after clicking the **Browse icon** to save the converted file.
5. Navigate to the **Start menu**. To modify the names of converted files, proceed as follows: click the Modify button, select a desired option from the Rename Options box, and finally click the Add button.

Use XMP files to Carry out your Tasks

In addition to RAW files, metadata sidecar files called XMP files are also present. They represent a conventional approach that can be employed to maintain modifications without impacting the initially generated RAW file. If you opt to manipulate your files in an alternative RAW image editor, the utilization of XMP files will facilitate the process of transferring between the different applications. XMP information can be read, saved, copied, and pasted when working with RAW files.

Read and Import Metadata in XMP Files

Metadata contained in XMP files can be imported and viewed by selecting RAW Metadata > To read metadata from the file, right-clicking on one or more RAW photo thumbnails on the Manage tab.

Save Changes in XMP Files

One or more RAW photo thumbnails can be right-clicked on the Manage pane to access the **RAW Metadata > Save Metadata** to File option. By doing so, it is possible to preserve any changes that are applied to XMP files. The procedure for copying and pasting data from one XMP file to another is as follows:

- Select the Manage pane using the right mouse button, and then right-click the thumbnail of the RAW image containing the required information.
- Navigate to the **Copy > RAW Metadata** option.
- Opt for one or more RAW image thumbnails to which you wish to apply the selected information.

- Right-click the thumbnails that you wish to copy and navigate to **RAW Metadata > Paste**.

CHAPTER FOUR

TRANSFERRING AND RETOUCHING PHOTOS

HOW TO TRANSFER IMAGES TO DIFFERENT APPLICATIONS

The proliferation of high-resolution digital cameras and scanners has caused the average file size of digital images to increase. These images require more memory to copy to the Windows Clipboard as opposed to pasting into another application.

By employing the Copy Special commands, one can optimize the process of transferring image data to office productivity software, including word processing, presentation, and e-mail applications. These instructions are accessible via the Edit menu.

DUPLICATE YOUR IMAGES FOR USE IN VARIOUS APPLICATIONS

The stages are as follows:

1. To commence, select **Edit > Copy Special**.
2. Select a command from the Copy Special submenu's available options:
   - Duplicate the current image on the clipboard at a resolution of 300 dots per inch (dpi) for printing purposes.
   - The Copy for Desktop Printing function duplicates the current image at a resolution of 200 DPI to the clipboard.
   - When you select Copy for Screen or Email, the current image will be saved to the clipboard in 96 dpi. This option is accessible by right-clicking the image. It is crucial to acknowledge that by selecting any of the three options from the submenu, the image depth will be converted to 8 bits per channel RGB and the extant image will be flattened to a single layer.
3. To paste the image, remember to press and hold the Ctrl and V keys on your keyboard while in the desired program.

4. Navigate to File > Save for Office to access a greater variety of options for resizing photos and choosing the file format when exporting them for use in other applications.

HOW TO ZOOM AND PAN

When images are accessed in PaintShop Pro, they are presented at a magnification level that ensures the visibility of the entire image within the workspace. This is the default configuration. To examine image details in greater detail, zoom in; to see more of the overall image, zoom out. Additionally, you can magnify a particular region of an image.

A portion of the image beyond the current visible window is visible. It is effortless to transition to a different region of an image while working at a high magnification level; no adjustment to the magnification level is required. This facilitates the optimization of one's productivity. If an image exceeds the dimensions of its window, navigation bars will be displayed on the right and bottom.

How to Zoom

The stages are as follows:

1. Choose the Zoom tool from the "**Tools**" toolbar.

2. To adjust the extent of the area, either click on it or right-click on it. By selecting the Zoom (%) option from the Tool Options panel, the specified percentage is reflected in the updated magnification level.

Additionally, you have the options to:

- Percentage enlargement: To achieve this, enter the desired value into the Zoom (%) control located on the Tool Options panel.

- Simply select "Zoom to 100%" from the Tool Options menu or select observe > Zoom to 100% to observe the image in its entirety.

When an image is zoomed in or out, the scale of the image window will be modified to accommodate the altered perspective. When utilizing the Zoom tool, users with a stylus or mouse with a scroll-wheel feature can alter the magnification. To adjust the magnification level of an image, navigate to the menu bar and select **View > Zoom in or View > Zoom out**.

How to Zoom in On a Section of an Image

The stages are as follows:

1. To enable the magnification mode, select the Magnifier option from the View menu.
2. Place the cursor over the specific region of the image that you desire to analyze in detail. 500% is the scale indicated for the area beneath the cursor.

3. To deactivate the magnifier mode, once more navigate to View > Magnifier from the menu bar.

How to Pan Around Your Image

The stages are as follows:

1. From the "**Tools**" toolbar, select the "**Pan**" tool.

2. Utilize the mouse to navigate the image.

There is also the opportunity for you to:

- To pan while using another tool, hold down the Spacebar while dragging with the alternative tool.

- Navigate effortlessly through an image using the Overview palette by dragging the preview rectangle to a different region.

Adjust the window to fit the image.

- Select "**Fit Image**" from the menu of the window.

- By selecting the Fit Window to Image icon from the Tool Options panel, one can effortlessly modify the window size of the Zoom or Pan tool to correspond with the image.

How to Undo and Redo Your Changes

You can undo a single action or multiple actions concurrently when editing an image. Any modifications you have applied to the image, such as adjustments to the colors, brushstrokes, or effects, can be undone. You have the option of redoing a single action or multiple actions to reapply undone instructions.

The image can also be restored to its most recently saved state. By utilizing the History palette, it is possible to reverse and redo actions uniquely, irrespective of their execution order.

It is important to note that specific operations, including file renaming, saving, opening and closing, Clipboard emptying, program-wide modifications, and the execution of non-pixel-editing directives, cannot be reversed via the **Undo control**.

Controls for Redo and Undo are Located on the History Palette

The History palette enables the simultaneous reversal of multiple actions, not just a single one. The History palette offers an exhaustive log of all operations executed on the image that is presently under consideration. The initial action is presented at the bottom of the sequence, followed by the most recent action. The History palette, as opposed to the reverse and Redo commands, provides the ability to reverse or redo operations regardless of their execution order.

A list of the 250 commands that were executed on the active image most recently is presented in the History palette. This is the default configuration. Individualize the Undo configuration to specify an increased or decreased quantity of undone instructions.

The controls for erasing and redoing previous actions on the History palette are delineated as follows:

- **Undo to Here:** The specified action and any succeeding actions are inverted when the Undo to Here command is executed. You will perform the identical action by selecting this option as you would by choosing the eye icon adjacent to an item. The unseen duties are represented by an unfilled box.
- **Redo to Here:** The specified action and any preceding undone actions are undone when the Redo to Here function is invoked. Selecting this option will produce the identical outcome as selecting the eye icon containing the yellow X.
- **Undo Selected:** The specified action is undone using the Undo selected function. Executing this operation is similar to holding down the Control key while selecting the eye indicator of an item. Cautiousness is crucial when reversing a particular action, as doing so could potentially impact subsequent outcomes.
- **Redo Selected:** This functionality allows users to undo a specific action that has been selected. Pressing this button is equivalent to selecting the red X-eye icon next to an item while holding down the Control key.
- **Clear Commands Selected to be Undone:** Once converted, commands that have been designated for undo are transformed into irreversible actions. Please affirm whether or not you wish to continue with this action.
- **Show Commands That Cannot Be Undone:** Displays or obscures the commands that are not reversible. When presented, items that are not reversible are denoted by a gray background.
- **History of an Empty Command:** Converts every item contained within the History palette into commands that cannot be undone. Please affirm whether or not you wish to continue with this action.

Undo an Action

- Select **Edit > Undo** from the menu bar to undo.
- To undo multiple actions concurrently, one can execute the **Edit > Undo function** iteratively. It is feasible to undo multiple actions that were

executed in the same sequence using the Undo command. By making use of the History palette, one can selectively undo previous actions.

- If the action in question is irreversible, the undo command will be rendered ineffective. To undo an action, press **Control + Z** or select the action from the Standard toolbar and then click the Undo icon.

Redo an Action

- Select Edit, followed by Redo.
- One action can be undone using the Undo command, whereas multiple actions can be undone in the same order using the Redo command. Users are provided with the ability to selectively undo actions via the History palette. To reverse an action, it is necessary to first undo it. You can utilize the **Ctrl + Alt + Z key** combination or the Redo icon on the Standard toolbar to revert an action.

- Return to the most recent version of the image that was saved. Upon selecting File > Revert, proceed.

Use the History Palette to Undo and Redo Actions

Select an action from the History palette and then navigate to any of the following options that appear:

- **Undo an action:** To undo an action, select the Undo to Here option or click the Undo/Redo icon. Unfilled boxes serve as representations of pending duties.
- **Redo an undone action:** To undo an action that has already been undone, navigate to the Redo to Here option or select the Undo/Redo icon. The selected action, in addition to all preceding actions, will be repeated in its entirety; its symbols will be updated to reflect the new state. It is imperative to bear in mind that any actions undone with a gray X preceding the one that was selected will not be restored. These

actions can solely be undone by employing the Redo Selected command.

- **Undo a specific segment of an action:** To undo a specific segment of an activity, press and hold the Control key while selecting the **Undo/Redo button** or the Undo Selected button corresponding to the selected action. Indicated by a gray X are operations that have been selectively undone.

- **Execute a partially undone action:** To reverse a partially undone action, select the Redo Selected button or click the reverse/Redo button while holding down the Ctrl key.

Adjust your Undo Settings

The stages are as follows:

1. From the menu bar, select "**File**," "**Preferences**," and "**General Program Preferences**."
2. Select the "**Undo**" option located in the panel on the left.
3. Before continuing, ensure that the checkbox designated "**Enable the undo system**" is selected. Ensure this box is checked to restore any modifications made to open images. After selecting OK, ensure that the checkbox is selected in the Preferences dialog box. It cannot be selected, and any changes made to an open image will not be reversible.
4. Select the appropriate options by checking or unchecking the matching boxes:

    - Limit undo/redo disk usage to a specified quantity of storage per open image; allows for the customization of hard disk storage allocated for undo/redo operations through the use of a control that accepts or modifies a value. Per open image, restrict the storage used for undo/redo operations. Availability of stowage space is contingent on the circumstances at hand. If your disk has a sufficient amount of unused space, you can bypass this option.

- Individuals are provided with the opportunity to modify the "Limit undo/redo to n steps per open image" configuration from its initial value of 250 steps. When the available capacity on the drive falls below 500 megabytes, the value indicated on the control will be reduced.
- By enabling Fast Redo, the Redo command can be configured to execute at the maximum speed feasible. To ensure that the Undo function operates swiftly, deselect this option before employing it.

5. Indicate the number of non-undoable steps that are retained once the Undo/Redo limit is reached by entering or establishing a value in the "**Non-undoable steps**" section of the History Palette control. 10 is the value by default.

6. Irreversible steps cannot be repeated or reversed. Reapplying them to the current image or other open images, copying them to the Clipboard, or saving them to a Quick script or standard PspScript file are all viable options.

HOW TO REPEAT A COMMAND

You can efficiently reapply a previously applied effect or correction using the Repeat command, eliminating the need to repeatedly return to the dialog box.

The Edit menu will always display the most recent command that is suitable for duplication. The Repeat command will be inaccessible if the preceding command cannot be repeated.

Here's how:

1. Select **Edit**, followed by **Repeat** from the menu.

2. By executing multiple instructions on each image via a script, the procedure can be simply automated. Simply hold down Shift while

selecting any toolbar icon or menu item to duplicate a command. When the repeated command is executed, the most recent configurations are implemented.

USING ADJUST

Capturing a multitude of images using a digital camera is a pleasurable and uncomplicated endeavor. However, there are situations in which the process of reviewing every single one, not to mention revising them, can be extremely taxing. By utilizing the **Adjust menu**, this undertaking can be elevated to a more enjoyable level. Standard editing operations such as cropping, straightening, color correcting, and eliminating red eyes and defects are within your capabilities.

You can assign stars to photographs that you deem unsuitable for your gallery. By employing this rapid editing technique, one can effectively finish the initial phase of photo modifications before focusing on a subset of images for more intricate adjustments.

What does the Adjust tab Signify?

By utilizing the controls situated in the Adjust menu, one can effortlessly access the tools and features of PaintShop Pro that are utilized most frequently.

To access the complete range of tools and features offered by the application in advanced editing mode, simply select the Edit tab located at the top of the application window. The image that was most recently viewed will now be the active image on the Adjust tab.

Activate the Adjust Tab

Individually modify images via the Adjust pane. Any modifications made when selecting a new instrument or feature are immediately implemented. Reversible adjustments can be made. While editing, feel at liberty to refer back to the original image. Selecting a thumbnail from the Organizer interface facilitates seamless transitioning to the subsequent image after the editing process is finished.

When prompted, you are presented with the choice between manually saving by enabling Autosave or setting it to occur automatically whenever you capture a new image.

Access the Adjust Tab in your Browser

Choose one of the following actions from the Adjust palette:

- When making adjustments to the image, choose a tool and meticulously refine the configurations. The modifications are implemented when an alternative tool or adjustment option is chosen, or when the Apply icon is clicked.

- Select the desired adjustment function by clicking on its name. The interface is utilized to modify controls. Upon selecting an alternative feature, the modifications will become effective.

Revert Modifications in the Adjust Section

Choose one of the alternatives provided:

- Navigate to the Undo icon located in the toolbar.

- To revert any modifications, ensure that the Reset button at the bottom of the Adjust window is clicked.

Using Depth Info to Choose Areas

In the case of cameras that record depth information (XDM metadata), the Adjust tab's Depth Selection function enables simple adjustments and the application of Instant Effects to particular regions of an image. A designated depth sensor on the camera determines the depth of the image based on the distance between the objects in the frame.

SELECT A POINT BASED ON THE DEPTH OF INFO

The stages are as follows:

1. To commence, navigate to the **Adjust tab**.
2. In the Organizer interface, utilize the Navigator tool to access an image containing depth information.
3. Select the Depth option from the Adjust panel.
4. To exhibit a selection marquee, ensure that the Enable Selection checkbox is selected.
5. Modify the selection distances by manipulating the markers along the Depth Range slider.
6. Choose a brush size by adjusting the Size slider, then utilize one of the following operations to refine your selection:
   - Select the desired region by delineating the circumference of the Preview area with your cursor after selecting the Add button.
   - To deselect regions from the Preview section, click Remove and then drag the cursor over the regions.
   - To reverse the selection, select the Flip Selection checkbox.

MANAGE TAB

By selecting the Manage pane, one can access the Navigation palette, Preview area, Organizer palette, and Info palette. Customization options for Manage include the ability to select between Preview and Thumbnail modes, modify the scale, relocate or conceal interfaces, and tailor display and file preferences to individual requirements.

Switch Effortlessly Between Preview and Thumbnail Modes

Select an option from the list located in the upper-right corner:

- In thumbnail mode, the Organizer palette content in the preview area is enlarged and secured.

- In preview mode, a substantial preview region of a solitary image is presented.

Adjust the Size of the Manage Tab Palettes

The stages are as follows:

1. When the cursor transforms into a two-way arrow, move it over the desired resizing border of the palette.

2. Simply drag to enlarge or reduce the size of the panel. The application effectively retains your most recent layout preferences during tab transitions and saves them automatically for the following session.

HIDE OR DISPLAY THE NAVIGATION PALETTE AND INFORMATION PALETTE

To access the Organizer palette, select one of the icons from the Organizer toolbar and click on it.

- To display or conceal the Navigation palette, toggle it.
- The visibility or opacity of information about an image can be adjusted through the Info palette.

- Easily and effectively minimize the Organizer palette (or any other palette) by pressing the **Auto Hide icon** located in the palette title bar.

BROWSE FOLDERS FOR YOUR IMAGES

By utilizing the Collections and Computer options within the Navigation interface, one can effortlessly traverse the computer-stored images.

- The Location of your physical and virtual folder libraries is indicated on the Collections pane. Similar to indexing, when files are imported to the catalog via the Collections page, it provides a simple method to browse and search for preferred images. It can be extremely beneficial to use file management tools, such as titles, descriptions, and ratings when searching for and organizing images. When necessary, you can effortlessly add or remove folders from the Collections page.
- Complete information regarding every folder present on your desktop and hard drive is presented in the Computer tab. Because these files are not imported to the catalog, tags, captions, and ratings from file management tools cannot be used to organize or search for photos viewed through the Computer pane. What advantages does utilizing the Computer tab provide? This approach facilitates the seamless transfer of files into the catalog from a location where their importation is currently not possible. Using the Computer tab to access images in folders containing numerous rarely-used files or files in transient folders is highly recommended.
- Upon selecting the folder in the Navigation palette, the images contained within it are presented as thumbnails in the Organizer palette. The formats and categories to be excluded from the cataloging procedure can be specified.

How to Access the Images in a Folder

The stages are as follows:

1. Choose one of the options from the Navigation palette that is displayed:
   - **Collections:** Provides an extensive enumeration of virtual collections in addition to a personalized catalog of folders.
   - **Computer:** Shows a list of all the folders and devices present on the system.
2. By double-clicking a folder, its subfolders can be viewed.

3. By selecting the folder containing the images you wish to view, you can select it.

The Organizer palette presents representations of all image files in the selected folder that are compatible. By selecting the minus sign in front of the name of a folder, the list of subfolders within that folder will be concealed.

Add a New Folder to the Collection Page

The stages are as follows:

1. The Collections tab can be accessed via the Navigation palette.
2. Select **Browse More Folders** from the folder list.
3. Click the OK button once the folder containing the images you desire to upload has been located. Ensure that you meticulously select your folder, as every subdirectory within it is structured differently. It is not advisable to include your profile folder or a root folder on your computer, as doing so can trigger superfluous cataloging.
4. By selecting the Make New Folder option from the Browse for Folder dialog window, one can effortlessly establish a fresh folder on the computer system.

Remove the Folder from the Collection Page

The stages are as follows:

1. To begin, navigate to the Collections tab within the Navigation palette.
2. By performing a right-click, one can delete a folder from the Folder display.
3. Select **Remove from List**.
4. The images contained within the folder will maintain their file management information (tags, ratings, captions) even after the folder is removed from the Collections page and the catalog. However, these particulars will no longer be searchable.

LOCATE IMAGES ON YOUR PC

The photographs are cataloged automatically in PaintShop Pro when they are imported and selected from the Navigation panel. Real-time filtering enables users to efficiently and effectively navigate through cataloged photographs by utilizing the Search field. There are several ways to locate photographs associated with particular dates: conduct a simple text search, utilize sophisticated search tools, or consult a calendar. It is possible to create a Smart Collection containing the search criteria and results obtained from an advanced search.

CONDUCT A QUICK SEARCH FOR IMAGES

Input a search term into the Navigation panel's Search field. Image details (EXIF or IPTC data), tags, captions, file names (including extensions), folder names (including drive letters), and drive letters are all valid search terms.

PERFORMING AN ADVANCED SEARCH

The stages are as follows:

1. The Collections tab can be accessed via the Navigation palette.
2. To access the list, click **Add Smart Collection** after double-clicking Smart Collections. Appearance of the Smart Collection dialog box.
3. Choose one of the following from the drop-down menu labeled "Find matching images":
    - **All:** Seek out photographs that adhere to all the prescribed guidelines.
    - **Any:** Search for photographs that meet any of the specified criteria.
4. From the initial drop-down menu on the left, select a search option.
5. To further specify your search, choose a search option from the following drop-down menu. A multitude of options will be presented in

the drop-down menu, contingent upon the search option selected in the preceding menu.
6. Enter or select a search term in the designated field. It is important to verify that the search term entered aligns with the search criteria chosen in the initial drop-down menu. To determine the ranking of an image, merely click the star quantity that corresponds to its rating.
7. Click **Preview** to view the file.
    - To incorporate a search rule, select the **Add Rule icon** situated in the dialog box's upper right corner.
    - To remove the most recent search criterion, simply select the Remove criterion option.
    - In the Smart Collection dialog box, select Save to save the search as a Smart Collection. Click the Save icon within the Save as Smart Collection dialog pane after entering a name. The collection is visible in the list of Smart Collections.

CHAPTER FIVE

PHOTO PERSPECTIVE AND LENS CORRECTION

CORRECTING PHOTOGRAPHIC PERSPECTIVE

When photographing wide or towering objects, perspective distortion can cause them to appear skewed or drooping. When the camera is not in direct alignment with the subject, distortion ensues.

Employing the Perspective Correction tool, rectify distortions of perspective, such as the inclined sides of a structure. The Pick tool enables the modification of a complete layer's perspective.

HOW TO CORRECT PERSPECTIVE IN PHOTOS

The stages are as follows:

1. Select the **Perspective Correction tool** by navigating to the Tools menu.

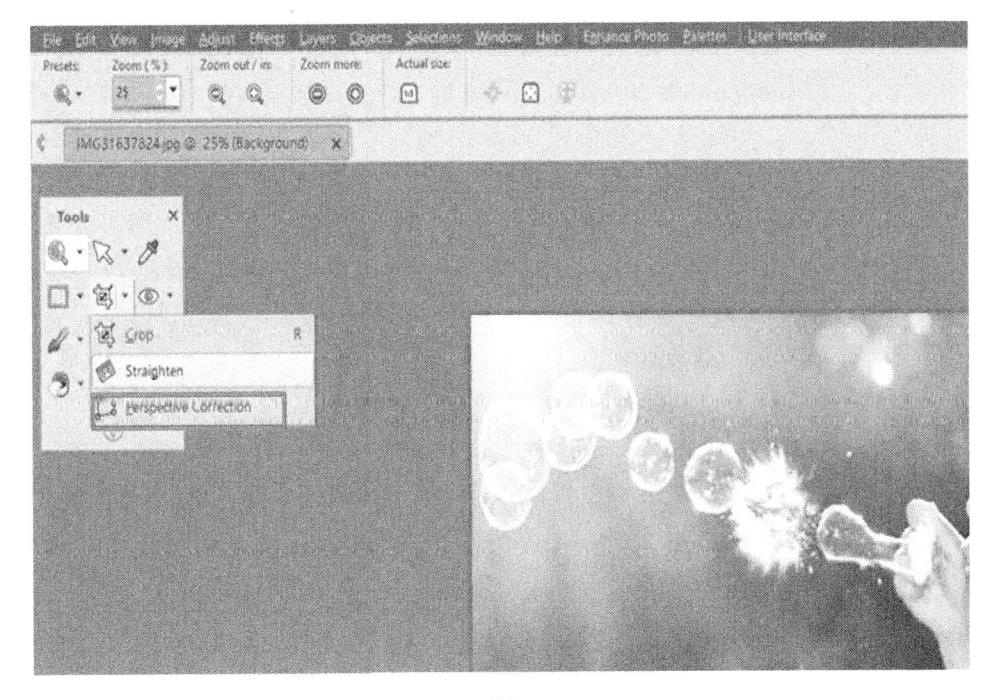

2. Select configurations for the controls that are exhibited in the Tool Options palette:
    - **Grid lines:** Configure or enter the desired quantity of gridlines.
    - **Crop image:** Following the application of perspective, the image is cropped to a rectangular shape. Remember to select the Crop image option to remove any portions of the image that extend beyond the rectangle.
3. Position every handle in a corner of the rectangular object.
4. Select "**Apply**" via the menu.

When the image is double-clicked, the specified command will be executed. In the Tool Options panel, select Cancel to return the perspective correction box to its initial rectangular form.

Precise Perspective in the Image Layer

The stages are as follows:

1. Utilizing the Layers panel, choose the layer that requires correction.
2. To get the gridlines displayed, click "**View Grid**." By utilizing the gridlines, you can coordinate the lines in your photographs that require horizontal or vertical alignment. After selecting View Change Grid, Guide & Snap Properties, the Grid page of the dialog box contains controls for modifying the grid's parameters.
3. Select the Pick tool by locating it within the Tools interface. By enlarging the image window, one can gain visibility to every corner handle associated with the current layer. To enlarge the image window, drag it inwards from a side or corner.
4. Utilizing the Ctrl key while dragging one of the corner handles, one can modify the dimensions of the designated layer. By releasing the drag, the image will be refreshed. Modify the perspective until the image appears flawless.

5. It is important to bear in mind that data recovery is possible through the enlargement of the image canvas if the correction results in certain image data being displaced beyond it.

HOW TO MAKE BASIC CHANGES TO THE IMAGE USING MECHANICAL TOOLS

You can make adjustments to a photo using either the One Step Photo Fix command or the Smart Photo Fix command if you are apprehensive about the optimal editing option. When you select the One Step Shot Fix option, your image will be automatically sharpened and color-balanced following a precise set of adjustments. It is advisable to utilize the Smart Photo Fix command to modify the adjustments made to the repairs before their finalization.

Apply basic corrections using Single/One Step Photo Fix

- Follow the One Step Photo Fix prompt by selecting Adjust.
- After a short interval of inactivity, your image is subjected to a series of critical alterations. The modifications are identical to those that would be implemented had the suggested configurations for the Smart Photo Fix function been endorsed.

- You can choose Edit > Undo if you are dissatisfied with the modifications made to your image. After that, choose Adjust Smart Photo Fix and modify the options that appear. It is worth investigating supplementary Adjust menu options, including Curves and Levels, which can be utilized to modify brightness and contrast.

HOW TO CORRECT ANY ISSUES USING SMART PHOTO FIX

The stages are as follows:

1. Select **Adjust** followed by **Smart Photo Fix**. The original image is displayed in the Before pane at the top of the dialog boxes.

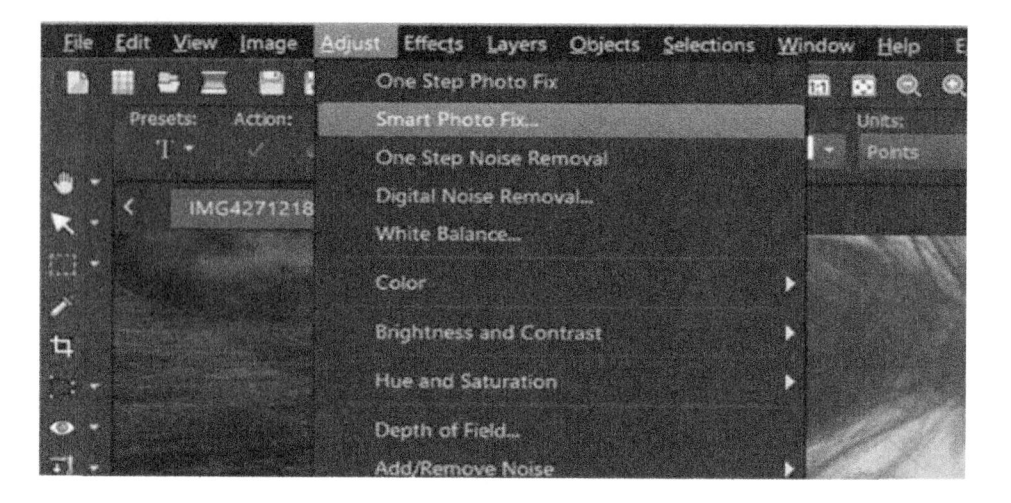

2. Remember to select the OK button when you have completed each task.

Furthermore, you are provided with the choice to:

- **Brighten or darken the images:** To adjust the brightness of the images, manipulate the sliders in the Brightness group box or input a value in the Overall, Shadows, and Highlights controls. Bear in mind that as values increase, luminosity decreases; conversely, negative values increase brightness.

- **Increase or reduce saturation:** To enhance or diminish saturation, manipulate the saturation level, utilize the slider, enter a value into the saturation control, or select an alternative saturation variety. It is important to note that making adjustments to parameters has the potential to either increase or decrease the vibrancy of colors.

- **Sharpen the photo's edges:** To enhance the definition of the photo's boundaries, modify the configurations within the Focus control through the entry of a value, the selection of a type, or the movement of the slider.

By choosing Suggest Settings or Reset to Default, users can effortlessly restore all settings to their initial values or the default configuration. To access the Smart Photo Fix feature's advanced settings, select the Advanced Options checkbox.

HOW TO USE THE ADVANCED FEATURES OF THE SMART PHOTO FIX

The stages are as follows:

1. Ensure that the Advanced Options checkbox is selected for the Smart Photo Fix option in the dialog box.

2. Remember to select OK when any of the duties in the table have been completed.

In addition, you can do the following:

- **Utilize sample points to balance colors:** It is essential to utilize sample points and verify the White Balance when balancing colors. The neutral black, gray, and white portions of the image are displayed in the Before window. Reminder: In certain images, the absence of black, gray, or white regions renders it impossible to identify sample points.
- **Discard the sample points present in the image:** Neglect the sample points and ensure that the White Balance checkbox is not selected. To restore the sampling points, re-check the corresponding option.
- **Delete a sampling point:** To remove a sampling point, select it from the preceding pane. Additionally, revisions will be implemented to the preceding and subsequent panels.
- **Darken the darkest pixels in the image:** Modify the Black slider to the right or input a value in the control adjacent to the slider to darken the darkest pixels in the image.

- **Lighten the photo's most pallid pixels:** Modify the White slider to the right or input a value in the control adjacent to the slider to adjust the photo's lightest pixels.

When including sample points, avoid using hues other than black, white, or gray to mitigate the risk of white balance complications. For example, avoid choosing a region that you are certain to be blue. Merely indicate which sections should be rendered in black, white, or gray.

LIGHTEN IMAGES

The discipline of photography frequently confronts lighting obstacles. In well-lit environments, photographs can acquire shadowy regions that lack sufficient detail. Adjust the exposure to accentuate the darker, underexposed regions of the image when the contrast between light and dark areas is excessively pronounced or the background is excessively dark. The intensity of a color can be modified through the adjustment of its saturation level.

How to Bring out the Best in your Images

The stages are as follows:

1. Select **Adjust > Flash Fill**.

2. Input the desired level of luminance for the darker regions using the Strength slider, which ranges from 0 to 100.

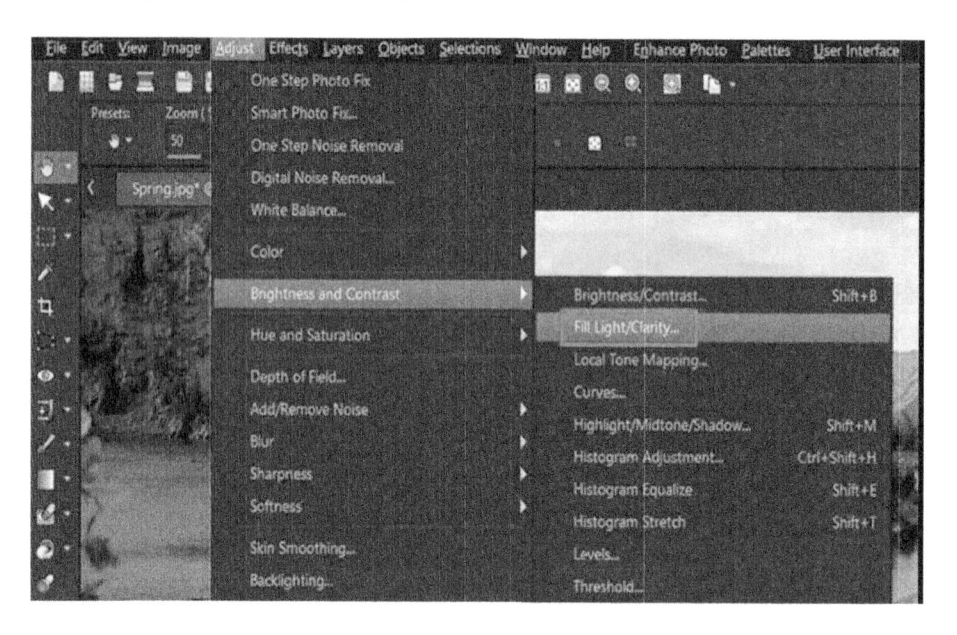

3. Input or type a value into the Saturation control to modify the image's overall color saturation. To increase saturation, one must employ values greater than zero, whereas to decrease saturation, one must utilize values greater than zero.

4. Click the OK button.

5. Don't forget to select **Adjust > Fill Flash** before adjusting backlighting if any areas of the image are excessively bright or dark.

DARKEN IMAGES

Excessive background light in photographs can occasionally completely detract from the image. Analogous issues manifest in photographs featuring an overabundance of flashes directed at the subject. The bright, overexposed regions of an image can be darkened through adjustment.

How to Darken Your Image

The stages are as follows:

1. Select **Backlighting** from the menu labeled Adjust.
2. In the Strength slider, enter a value between 0 and 100 to modify the darkness of the lighter portions.
3. Input or modify a value in the Saturation control to ascertain the color saturation of the image. Saturation increases when values are greater than zero, and decreases when values are greater than zero.
4. Click the OK button.
5. Choose **Adjust > Fill Flash** before **Adjust > Backlighting** if there are areas in your image that are excessively bright or dark.

REMOVING THE PURPLE RUFFLES

In digital images, purple halo rings surrounding overexposed portions of a color shot are common. Fringing can become a conspicuous issue when a photograph features a bright sky in the background and light purple halos emanate from the subject's edges. Resolve the problem with your image by utilizing PaintShop Pro .

ELIMINATING DIGITAL NOISE

The term "**noise**" is employed in photography to denote minute color specks that have the potential to obstruct the image's clarity. Poor lighting conditions or sensor malfunctions in digital cameras are frequently the root causes of these specks. When magnifying an image depicting a clear blue sky, for instance, specks of green, orange, red, purple, or other hues can become visible.

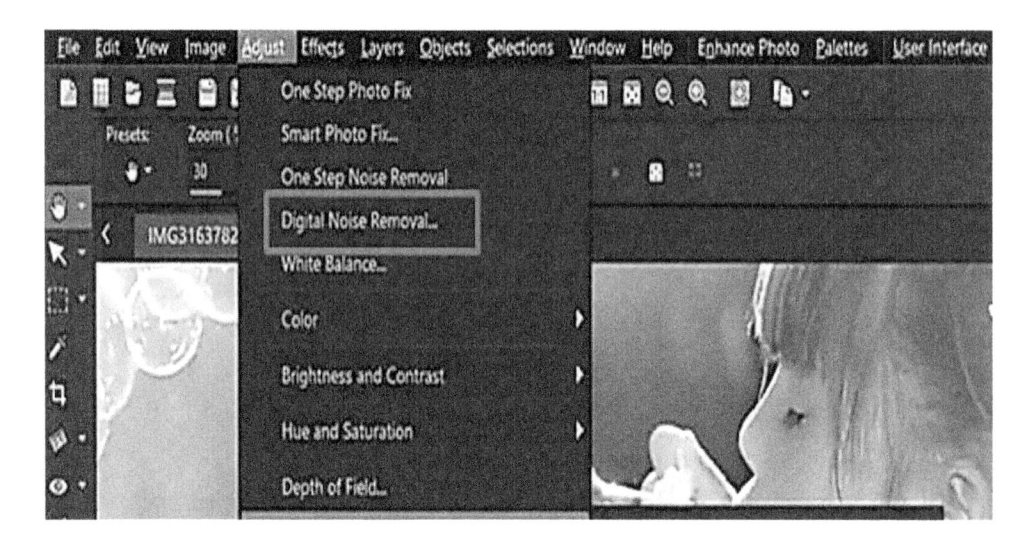

You have access to three potent noise removal tools in the PaintShop Pro toolkit: One Step Noise Removal, AI Denoise, and Digital Noise Removal. The noise reduction command initiates an analysis of the image by the software, which identifies and rectifies noise artifacts while maintaining the image's critical edge characteristics.

- **One-Step Noise Removal:** The One Step Noise Removal command enables the expeditious application of noise reduction to a given shot.
- **Artificial Intelligence denoise (AI):** Analyze and reduce noise in your images using artificial intelligence. By selecting Enhanced, the noise reduction level can be modified.
- Digital noise removal enables precise regulation of remedy applications.

REMOVING DIGITAL NOISE COMMAND

By effectively eliminating digital camera noise with the Digital Noise Removal command, you can improve the quality of your photographs. Images captured using a single camera often display noise in uniform regions. To guarantee uniformity throughout these photographs, contemplate developing a preset.

In the following circumstances, this command can prove to be the most efficacious course of action:

- Employing the command with reduced parameters can effectively augment the overall image sharpness while preventing excessive blurring, particularly when dealing with images that contain substantial amounts of noise, as in the case of a video whiteboard clip.
- Implement this command exclusively on critical regions of images captured using standard settings, such as image flaws encircling the subject.

- Establish the color ranges within images that will determine which segments are incorporated or excluded during the noise reduction procedure. You might, for instance, elect not to retouch the skin tones in a photograph. Multiple definitions of these protected areas are permissible.

RAPIDLY REMOVING DIGITAL NOISE

Tap **Adjust** followed by **One-Step Noise Removal**. The noise ceases spontaneously following a brief interval.

Use AI Denoise for Noise Analysis and Removal

The stages are as follows:

1. To begin, navigate to **Adjust > AI Denoise**.

2. Select one of the options listed below:

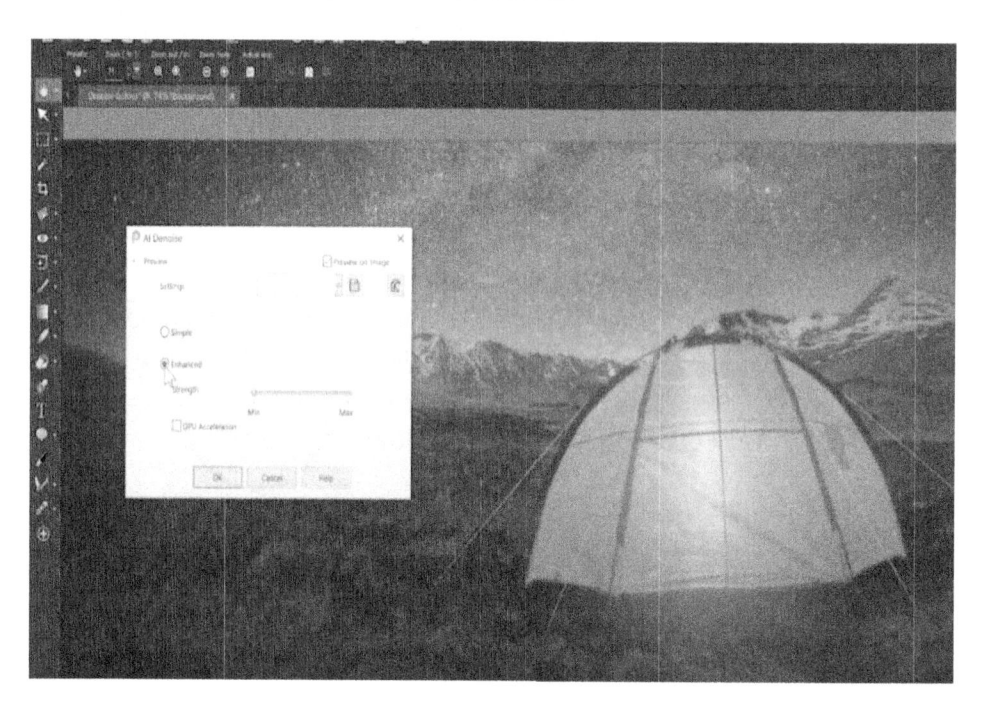

- Select **Simple** for a quick repair option.
- Select the **Enhanced** option and manipulate the Strength slider to regulate the extent of denoise implementation. Ensure that

the GPU Acceleration checkbox is selected if you are aware that the GPU can be used to accelerate processing.

3. Click OK, and use the green bar at the bottom of the program window to monitor the progress of the AI analysis.

HOW TO PROTECT IMAGE AREAS FROM NOISE CORRECTIONS

The stages are as follows:
1. In the Adjust menu, choose **Digital Noise Removal**.
2. Navigate to the Protect Image tab.
3. Modify the perspective in the Before pane by employing magnification and panning to concentrate on the region that requires protection.
4. Select the protected area while maintaining the Ctrl key down. In the Remove Noise tabbed section of the image window, holding down Ctrl does not cause a crosshair to emerge.
5. Modify the values in the Selected hue range group box of the Hue and Range controls. The sampled area is precisely reflected by the current parameters. The color dial can be modified by angling it within the ring.
6. In the Protect selected hue range group box, modify the handles on the graphs to lessen the amount of correction and flattening that is applied to the hue range segment. To illustrate, the middle tone of the specified color range is removed from the graph by relocating the middle handle to the lowermost position.

7. Select OK. By selecting **Reset Current**, any color adjustments executed for a particular color range will be nullified. To undo all color adjustments, select **Reset All**.

DELETE CHROMATIC ABERRATIONS IN THE IMAGE

Chromatic aberration occurs when the image captured by the camera exhibits colors that are not precise. In conventional film cameras, a faulty lens frequently causes chromatic aberration. Chromatic aberration in digital cameras can arise due to a multitude of factors, some of which are delineated as follows:

- The lens aberration of the camera can contribute to the appearance of blurriness at the image's periphery. Chromatic aberrations can potentially affect images produced using telephoto and zoom lenses, as digital cameras are designed to capture light beams that are at a considerable distance from the optical axis.
- Sensor blooming can occur due to the auto-exposure function of the camera, which computes the accurate exposure setting.
- Diverse colors are captured by distinct camera sensor components; these colors can combine to form a solitary pixel. The term for this process is demosaicing. The camera is capable of performing internal operations such as sharpening, noise reduction, and artifact removal following processing.

REMOVE CHROMATIC ABERRATIONS IN YOUR PHOTOS

Follow these steps:

1. **Chromatic Aberration Removal** can be accessed via the Adjust menu.
2. Verify that the Before and After panes of the dialog box are positioned at the top.
3. Increase the magnification level of the dialog pane by a minimum of 200%. Beside the magnification knob are the Before and After panes, respectively. A 200% magnification can assist in more precisely identifying flaws in a photograph.
4. To generate a visible image region in the Before pane, navigate the image while clicking the Pan button.
5. Using the dragging function, determine the region in the Before window that needs to be corrected. A reminder: The area requiring correction is denoted by the sample box. A maximum of ten sample cartons can be produced. Each sample box in the List of Samples portion located at the

dialog box's center is designated with the notation "**Sample n**" (where n represents a numerical value ranging from 1 to 10). A color swatch is appended to the left of each sample listing, representing the mean color of the area that was sampled.

6. Choose an entry from the List of Samples to serve as an example.
7. Determine the pixel range of the active sample by inputting a value into the Range control or modifying it accordingly to determine the color range. Above the Range control, a color box indicates the specified range.
8. Determine the magnitude of the aberration in the sample by inputting or encoding a value into the Radius control. Keep in mind that 10 is the preset value. In general, values within the range of 4 to 20 are deemed acceptable. In the context of sampling regions exhibiting sensor blooming aberrations, values exceeding 10 can prove advantageous. When mitigating aberrations of one or two pixels caused by demosaicing or working with images less than one megapixel in size, values falling below 10 can prove advantageous. Minimally adjust the Radius control to achieve the desired correction for the aberration.
9. Select "**Okay**."

DISTORTION

Distortion can be present in lenses with fixed focal lengths, but zoom lenses that offer an extensive spectrum of focal lengths generally manifest greater lens distortion. When the image is magnified unevenly from the edges to the center, barrel, and pincushion distortions result.

A barrel distortion occurs when the lens magnification is decreased at the margins of an image, resulting in a rounded appearance. Pinch or constriction of an image's sides is referred to as pincushion distortion. The correction of lens-specific barrel and pincushion distortion can be achieved through the analysis of a sequence of photographs taken at various focal lengths. Profiles are available for a wide range of lens and camera combinations in Corel PaintShop Pro.

VIGNETTING

Produced by various elements, including optics (specifically, the lens), the sensor (which can exhibit reduced sensitivity to light when positioned at an angle), and additional elements like filters or lens shields that obscure the periphery of an image. Vignetting, or the discoloration of an image's margins, is caused by light loss.

By sharpening the borders of an image, vignetting can be diminished. Photographers frequently employ vignette effects to direct attention to the primary subject matter of their images. Lens Correction can introduce or remove vignetting. Vignetting is consistently applied to the cropped region of an image. When correcting a vignette, nevertheless, the complete original frame is employed. To resolve concerns, one can choose to employ either Manual or Automatic controls.

By utilizing the pre-installed camera and lens profiles in PaintShop Pro, automatic corrections can be applied to your images.

- To enable or disable correction, toggle the Lens Correction option.
- The image is enlarged to suit the image frame via automatic cropping.
- If a picture contains information, the camera manufacturer will automatically display it; otherwise, you can configure it manually.
- If the image contains information, the camera model drop-down menu will appear automatically; alternatively, you can configure it manually.
- **Lens drop-list:** Indicates, if metadata is available, the lens that was utilized to acquire the image. It is important to note that the software can select the closest match at random, contingent upon the available data. Errors can be rectified by selecting the appropriate camera model, manufacturer, and lens from the provided lists. These factors ascertain the optimal profile for distortion reduction.

- **Focal Length:** If an image contains data, the focal length setting of the lens employed during the capture process will be displayed, or it can be adjusted manually.

Correction settings can be specified manually as opposed to utilizing correction parameters derived from profiles established within the application. This feature proves advantageous for lenses that have yet to be incorporated into the lens correction database.

The utilization of these controls is critical in rectifying chromatic aberration.

- R/C—manages the transition of colors along the Red/Cyan axis.

- B/Y — This parameter denotes the color conversion along the axis of blue and yellow.

The vignette correction comprises the following elements:

- **Vignette correction:** A straightforward selection toggles the **vignette correction** on or off. Alternative lens correction methods do not affect this setting.
- **Strength:** The magnitude of the correction determines whether it is luminous (positive or right) or black (negative or left).
- **Radius:** The profundity of the adjustment within the image is specified by this parameter.

USING LENS CORRECTION

1. Select one of the options provided:
    - Access the Lens tab for RAW images by opening the image in the Camera RAW Lab.
    - To rectify the lens on JPEG and TIFF images, select Adjust.

2. Select the desired mode (Manual or Automatic) and modify the parameters accordingly.

Exploring Various Forms of Lens Distortion

In the process of investigating different types of lens distortion, PaintShop Pro identifies and corrects three prevalent types that cause straight lines to appear curved.

- **Barrel distortion:** an apparent protrusion of the image's center. It is essential to align the axis of the camera lens with the center of the image to rectify distortion effectively.
- **Fisheye distortion:** The image exhibits an elongated appearance as if it were encircled by a sphere or distended. The margins of the photograph appear to be distorted.

- **Pincushion distortion** is a visual effect in which the center of the image seems to be inwardly pressed.

Correcting Barrel Distortion

The stages are as follows:

1. Under Adjust, select **Barrel Distortion Correction**.
2. Identify any curved contours within the image and manipulate the Strength parameter to rectify their angle.
3. Then, press OK.

Using adding or removing pixels, it is possible to modify the scale in the center of the image by checking the box labeled Preserve central scale. The Result Size group box exhibits modifications made to the width and height of the original image.

Correcting the Fish-eye Distortion

Proceed as follows to rectify fish-eye distortion:

1. Fisheye Distortion Correction can be selected from the Adjust menu.
2. To delete distortion, adjust the Field of View control to the appropriate value.
3. Then, press OK.

It is important to modify the scale in the image's center by performing pixel additions or removals while selecting the Preserve central scale option. The Result Size group box exhibits modifications implemented on the dimensions of the original image.

Correct the Pincushion Distortion

Proceed with the following steps:

1. Step one is to select **Pincushion Distortion Correction** from the Adjust menu.
2. Identify curved lines within the image and modify their straightness by inputting a numerical value or adjusting the Strength control.
3. Then, press OK.

CHAPTER SIX

WHITE BALANCE

HOW TO ADJUST WHITE BALANCE

Frequently, editing the hues of an image can result in a significant improvement. An assortment of illumination conditions, camera models, and camera processing can result in erroneous image coloration. Image scans might manifest atypical color casts.

Employ the diverse color-balancing functionalities available in PaintShop Pro to remove any undesired color tints from your image and generate hues that appear natural.

By adhering to the provided guidelines, the following operations can be executed on either a section or the complete image:

- Achieve a seamless color balance in a photograph while preserving its overall luminosity.

- Modify the proportionate hue of the channel's red, blue, or green components.
- Increase the contrast and vibrancy of images that are vanishing.
- Produce a photographic negative by converting the colors of each pixel to their inverses. To illustrate, substitute yellow for blue, black for white, yellow for blue, white for black, and so forth.
- Modify the relative proportions of red, green, and blue in the image to alter the overall color cast.

The stages are as follows:

1. **White Balance** can be selected from the Adjust menu.
2. Ensure that the Smart White Balance option is selected. PaintShop Pro is capable of performing image analysis and automated minor adjustments.
3. To achieve warmer colors, move the temperature slider to the right; to achieve frigid colors (more blue) or orange, move it to the left.
4. Select OK.

By selecting the Advanced Options checkbox and modifying the temperature values in the White Balance settings, one can precisely calibrate the image's tonal balance following the preferred color temperature. Color modifications are possible by adjusting the Temperature and Tint values in the Enhance White Balance group box.

HOW TO MIX COLOR CHANNELS

Follow the following steps:

1. Select **Channel Mixer** from the section labeled "**Adjust Colors**."
2. Select one of the alternatives provided:
    - Select a color channel from the drop-down menu labeled "Output channel" to manipulate and maintain the color image.

- Select the Monochrome alternative to convert the image to monochrome, which is analogous to grayscale but possesses 16 million color depths. Gray appears in the output channel drop-down menu.

3. Modify the color proportions within the channel through slider adjustments or by inputting values into the corresponding controls labeled "Red," "Green," and "Blue" in the Source Channels group box. The quantity of crimson in the image that was originally present has been decreased by half. For instance, in the context of modifying the Red channel, configure the Red control to 50%.
4. Modify the Constant variable as necessary. The variable is initially configured to a value of zero. Modify the toggle to reduce the intensity of the color channel. To enhance the luminance of the color channel, adjust the slider.
5. Select "**Okay**."

Restore the Colors that have Lost their Vibrancy

The stages are as follows:

- Select the option labeled "Adjust Color Fade Correction." To locate the critical area of an image, such as the face, move the center by dragging within the Before pane.
- Make adjustments to the "**Amount of corrective control**" value to achieve a more natural appearance for the image. 45 is the default value. Employ the minimum quantity necessary to achieve a satisfactory adjustment. Prolonged corrections have the potential to induce object blending and can lead to a loss of clarity in shadow regions.
- Select OK.

How to Adjust the Color Cast

Follow the following steps:

- Select **Red/Green/Blue** in the section labeled "**Adjust Colors**."
- Alter the color balance by adjusting the values in the red, green, and blue parameters, respectively. The initial value remains unaltered in the absence of any value. Apply a whole number to intensify the color. With the aid of a negative integer, reduce a fraction of the hue. Changing the intensity of blue yields a yellow hue, while adjusting the intensity of green generates a magenta hue, and adjusting the intensity of red generates a cyan hue.
- Select OK.

Adjust the Contrast, Brightness, and Clarity.

Make adjustments to the luminosity, contrast, and clarity of your images with PaintShop Pro . Contrast denotes the disparity between the brightest and darkest pixels in an image. By analyzing contrast in particular regions, the level of image detail can be modified.

By adhering to the provided guidelines, the following operations can be executed on either a selection or the complete image:

- Manually adjust the contrast and luminance configurations
- Ensure that the subject is in sharp focus and that the photograph is clear to achieve this.
- Modify the luminance setting for every individual photograph.
- Make necessary adjustments to the highlights, mid-tones, and shadows to attain seamless transitions between tones.
- Modify the exposure configuration
- Ensure that the luminance values of the pixels are uniformly distributed throughout the entire luminosity spectrum, spanning from black to white.

- To rectify the histogram's failure to encompass the complete luminance spectrum, modify the overall contrast.
- Modify the image's luminance, contrast, and gamma values.

- Produce an exclusively black-and-white photograph

HISTOGRAMS

A histogram can be employed to assess the tonal range of an image and make adjustments to how highlights, mid-tones, and shadows are distributed. In essence, the histogram serves as a visual indicator to determine whether an image has been appropriately exposed, underexposed, overexposed, or a combination of the two.

Histograms are often presented on the LCD of digital cameras, and certain models allow users to modify the histogram of the scene before image capture. The dialog box of numerous PaintShop Pro functions exhibits the histogram. These alternatives include Histogram Adjustment, Curves, Levels, and the sophisticated mode of Smart Photo Fix.

When analyzing a histogram, it is critical to consider the following:

- Indicated on the left-hand side of the histogram is the quantity of black or nearly black pixels present in the image.

- The quantity of white or nearly white in the image is denoted on the right-hand side of the histogram.

The Histogram Adjustment dialog box exhibits the pixel count associated with each channel value that has been selected on the graph. The maximum number of pixels on the graph is represented along the vertical axis, which spans from zero to one. The value of the chosen channel, which is between 0 and 255, is represented along the horizontal axis. To instantly observe the histogram associated with a given image, navigate to **View > Palettes > Histogram**.

Make Adjustments to either the Contrast or the Brightness

The stages are as follows:

1. Adjustments can be made under **Brightness/Contrast** after selecting **Brightness and Contrast**.

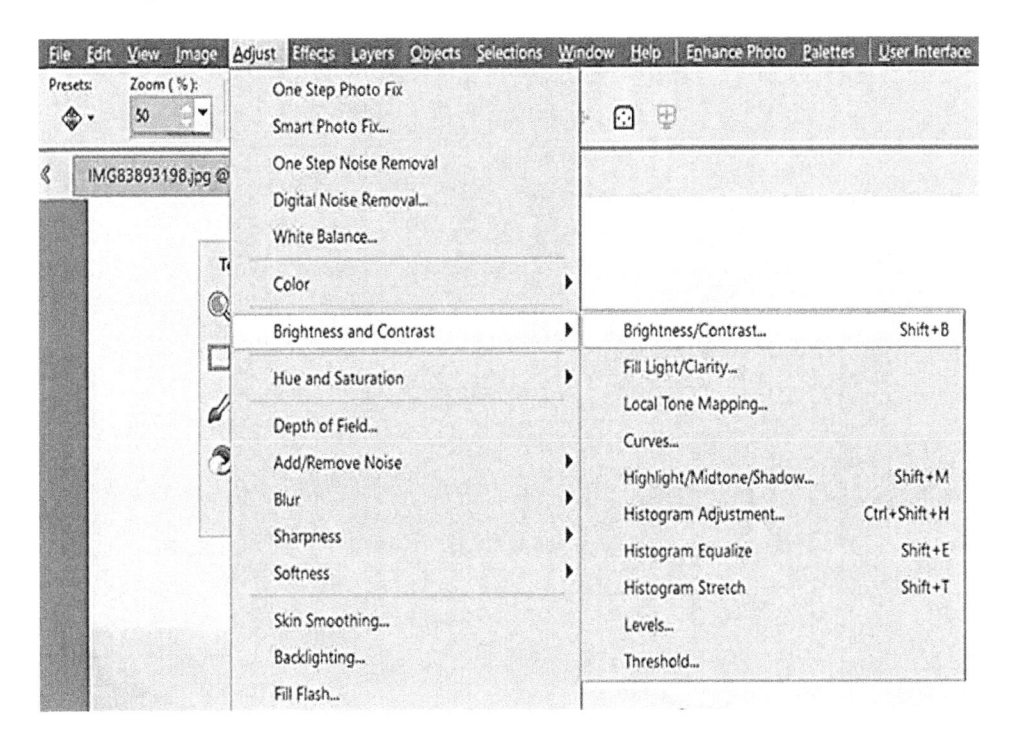

2. Please enter a letter or number into the Brightness control. Negative values obliterate the image, whereas positive values amplify it. Zero preserves the current value.

3. Enter a value or modify it directly through the Contrast control. Negative numbers diminish contrast, whereas positive numbers augment it. Zero preserves the initial configuration of the setting.

4. Adjust the image's appearance using the magnification control in the dialog box after clicking OK in the Before and After panes.

Lighten up the Dark Areas and the Clarity

The stages are as follows:

1. In the tab labeled "Adjust Brightness and Contrast," select **Fill Light/Clarity**.

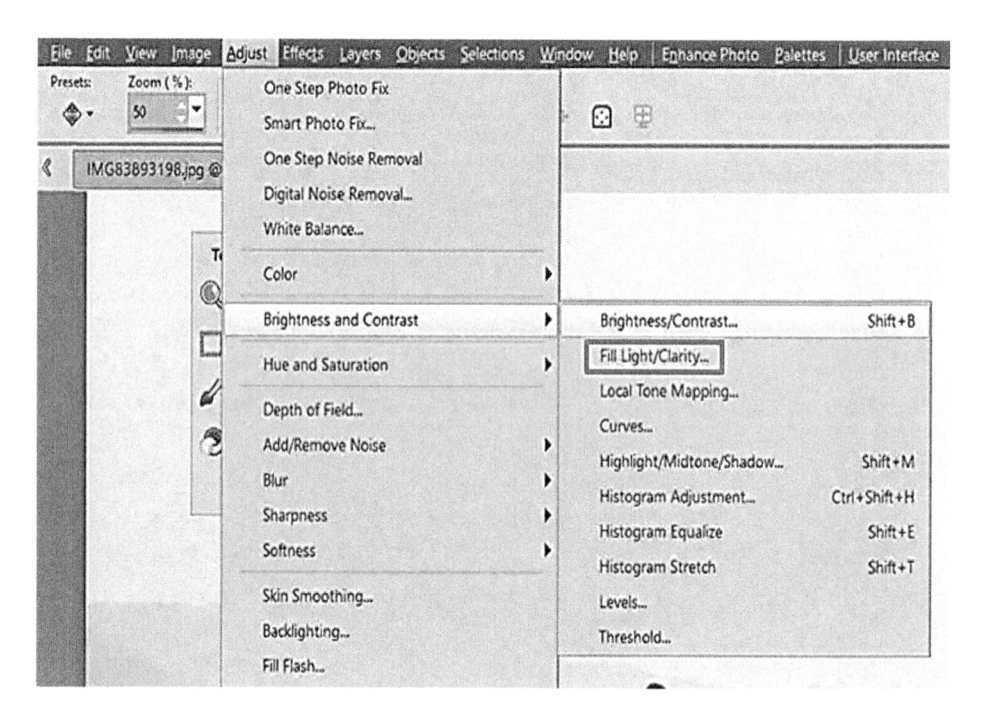

2. Enter text or a value into the Fill Light control. By augmenting the values, the image's darkest regions are illuminated, while the other parameters remain unchanged at zero.
3. Continue by entering a letter or value into the Clarity control. Negativity narrows the focus, whereas positivity illuminates more information. Zero preserves the current value.
4. Click the OK button.

Enhancing Both the Depth and the Clarity

Follow the following steps:

1. **Local Tone Mapping** can be selected under the Adjust Brightness and Contrast menu.
2. Enter or input a value into the Strength control. Employ the bare minimum required to attain a satisfactory outcome. Elevated values have the potential to introduce undesired anomalies into an image.
3. Adjust the image's appearance using the magnification control in the dialog box after clicking OK in the Before and After panes.

How to Modify the Brightness of the Color Channels

The stages are as follows:

1. In the tab labeled "Adjust Brightness and Contrast," select **Curves**.
2. Channel color selection via the Channel drop-down menu:
    - **RGB** adjustment function allows for the modification of the red, green, and blue channels of a composite histogram.
    - **Red**—Allows modifications solely to the red channel.
    - **Green** - Exclusively permits editing of the green channel.
    - **Blue** – Allows exclusive modification of the blue channel.
3. Modify the correlation between the input levels (original pixel brightness) and the output levels (corrected pixel brightness) by adjusting the graph's data points. The pixel luminance values are visually represented in the upper-left corner of the histogram graph as the curve points are modified. The input value is represented on the left, while the output value is depicted on the right.
4. Click the OK button.

You are presented with the chance to elevate it to a higher degree:

- **Add a point into the curve:** To insert a point, click on the designated location on the curve. It is important to note that an additional point can be added to the curve to modify its form.

- **Remove the point from the curve by dragging it onto the graph**: To remove a point from the curve, precisely relocate the active curve point using the Arrow keys.
- **Automatic contrast adjustment:** To modify the contrast of the image, click the Contrast button in the Auto group box. Select this option if you are content with the colors in the image but wish to increase the contrast.
- **Automatically adjust the white balance of the image:** To modify the white balance of the image, select the Color option within the Auto group box. A reminder: By pressing this icon, the black and white elements in the image will be automatically located.
- **Automatically change the contrast and color:** In the Auto group box, select the Levels icon to automatically adjust the contrast and color.
- **Set your black, and white point and insert the dropper:** Select the desired black, gray, or white point, and subsequently enable the dropper by checking the Dropper Color option. Subsequently, positioned within the Before panel, select an area that you are certain to be white, gray, or black. An update is made to the After pane and, if the Preview on Image checkbox is selected, the image window as well.
- **Automatically determine the appropriate black or white point**: To ascertain the appropriate black, gray, or white point, hover the cursor in the Before pane while holding Alt. As one hovers over regions classified as medium, light, and dark, the corresponding color pipette will activate.
- **Choose histogram clipping limits for the auto contrast and color buttons:** To configure the histogram clipping limits for the levels, color, and auto contrast buttons, navigate to the Options menu. Select the corresponding percentage values for the lower limit, upper limit, and strength controls within the dialog box labeled "Auto color Options." When modifying the upper and lower limit controls, it is important to note that higher values will yield more robust automated settings, whereas lower values will result in less robust automatic settings. In addition, diminished strength values lead to a reduction in shearing.

- **Restore all modified values to their original values:** To restore all modifications to their initial states, select the Reset icon situated close to the color pipette. A button labeled "Reset to default" is situated close to the "Save presets" button.

Remember to modify the image view in the Before and After panes by utilizing the zoom control in the dialog box.

HOW TO ADJUST THE MID-TONES, HIGHLIGHTS, AND SHADOWS

The stages are as follows:

1. From the Adjust menu, select Highlight/Midtone/Shadow, followed by Brightness and Contrast.
2. Select one of the options listed below:
    - The absolute correction approach entails positioning the 25% histogram point (Shadows), 50% histogram point (Midtones), and 75% histogram point in their corresponding positions. The customary values for the photograph's shadow, midtone, and highlight are approximately 35, 50, and 65, respectively. Zones of light and darkness represent variations in value.
    - Improving lightness levels by employing the relative adjustment method following their initial conditions. A value decreases to darken the area, whereas an increase in value illuminates it.
3. Input values into the Highlight, Shadow, and Midtone controls.
4. Remember to modify the image's appearance in the Before and After panes using the zoom control in the dialog box after selecting OK.

How to Correct Exposure by Using a Histogram

The stages are as follows:

1. In the Adjust menu, navigate to the Brightness and Contrast tab and select **Histogram Adjustment**.

2. Select one of the alternatives from the list in the Edit group box:
   - **Luminance:** Modify the luminosity levels of the image to achieve appropriate contrast in luminance.
   - **Colors:** Colors afford the user the ability to choose a color channel that is modifiable. It is crucial to choose a color from the drop-down menu when utilizing the Colors option.
3. Select **Default** from the Load Preset drop-down menu. By default, the image is not altered in any way.
4. Adjust the Low toggle. Observe for a space on the histogram's left side between the initial value and the point at which the graph commences to ascend. The absence of a crevice indicates that the pixels depicting the darkest areas are not entirely black. At the point where the graph begins to ascend, move the Low slider (the black triangle). When the Low control is engaged, the position is within the lower range of values (0–254). The proportion of pixels whose contrast is lost as a consequence of being between zero and the low value is indicated by the bottom control. Ensure that the Low value, which serves as a benchmark, remains below 0.1%.
5. Modify the values on the High slider. Ensure that a space exists between the right window edge and the point at which the graph descends to zero pixels on the histogram's right side. If present, move the High slider (white triangle) to any space on the graph. This operation causes the image's lightest pixels to become white. It is imperative to maintain the High value below 0.1% as a baseline principle.
6. Modify the values on the Gamma slider. Gamma adjustment is of the utmost importance when working with images that are excessively dark or light. By increasing the gamma by one, the image's luminosity can be improved. Modify the Gamma adjuster situated to the right. By shifting the Gamma slider to the left, the image will become darker.
7. Modify the values on the Midtones slider. It is crucial to apply mid-tone compression to diagrams containing low points in the middle and peaks at the margins. Shadows and highlights can be enlarged to unveil concealed information. When subjects are positioned too near to the camera on a dark background, they will be excessively illuminated. To

compress the midtones, manipulate the Midtones slider. To modify the midtones, descend the Midtones slider when the graph exhibits a central peak accompanied by a reduced number of pixels on the periphery.

8. To generate artistic effects, modify the Output Max and Output Min settings on the histogram's left-hand side and click OK. A black circle symbolizes the Minimum slider, while a white circle signifies the Maximum slider, both of which are contained within the gray square. By reducing the value of the Max slider, the image's lightest pixels will become darker. To enhance the brightness of the image's darkened pixels, raise the Min slider. Despite vertical slider adjustments, the horizontal axis is influenced by the maximum and minimum values (which span from 0 to 255). Beyond the range, every pixel is adjusted to suit it. Modifications can be implemented by selecting an alternative color component from the Edit drop-down menu.

Expanding the Histogram and Contrast

Select Histogram Stretch from the Adjust > Brightness and Contrast menu.

The Histogram Stretch command is utilized to transform the darkest pixel into black and the lightest pixel into white. Images containing the complete spectrum from black to white are unaffected by this command. If the pixels in the original image are nearly black and white, the effect of this command will be negligible. This command will substantially improve original images that are exceedingly dull and deviate from black and white.

CHAPTER SEVEN

HUE AND SATURATION

HOW TO ADJUST THE HUE AND SATURATION

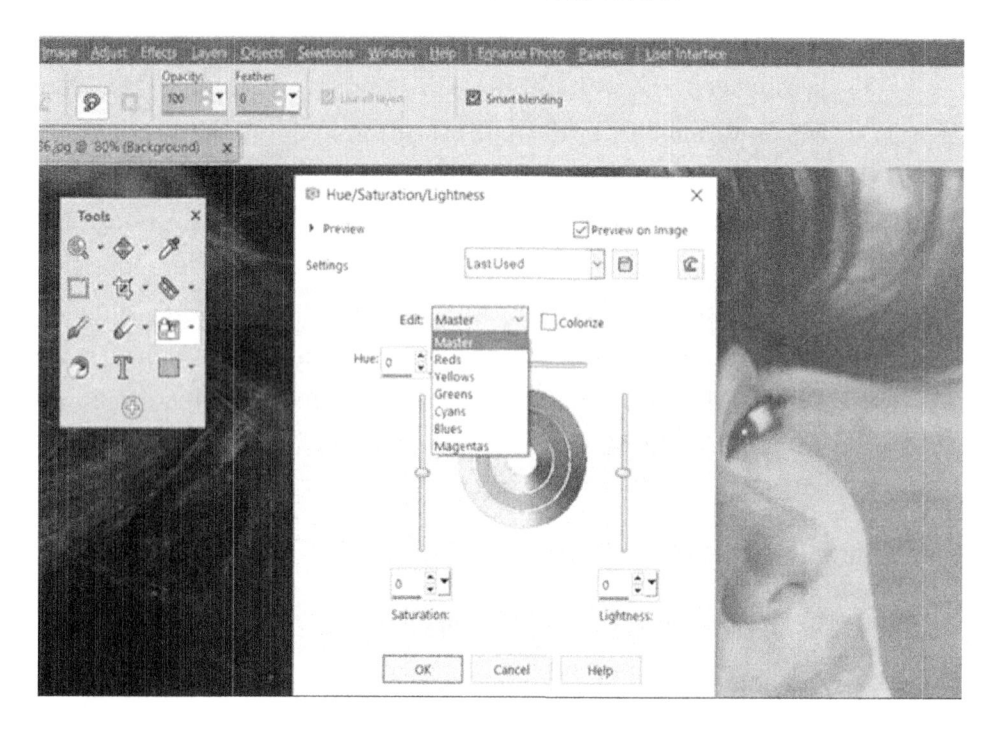

The absence of white in a color signifies its saturation level, which serves as an indicator of its purity or vibrancy. An entirely saturated color does not contain any white. A color exhibiting a saturation value of 0 percent is commonly perceived as possessing a grayish tint. The quality that distinguishes one color from another is called the tint.

A hue is a descriptive term for the actual color, such as yellow or red. The vibrancy of a color is determined by the intensity of its saturation. Consider the vivid orange color, which is renowned for its high level of saturation. By decreasing the saturation value without editing the hue or luminance, the orange hue undergoes a series of transitions: from a brownish hue to taupe, and ultimately to a neutral gray when the saturation is set to zero.

By decreasing the saturation level, the color is eliminated, leaving behind only the grayscale component. Taupe and mauve are regarded as having a low saturation level owing to their delicately colored, neutral tones. Yellow bananas and red fruits are hues characterized by high saturation. The measure of a hue's saturation is the amount by which it differs from a grayscale representation of the same intensity.

By increasing the saturation of digital photographs, one can achieve vivid hues and a visually arresting effect. However, excessive application can result in color distortion and undesirable skin tones. Apply the Vibrancy control to concentrate on particular regions of the image that have low saturation without affecting the remainder of the image. It is possible to augment the hue in particular regions of an image that possess comparatively low saturation, without substantially modifying the complexion.

Four options are available in PaintShop Pro for modifying the saturation and chroma of an entire image or a selection:

- It is feasible to substitute every color with a single hue and manipulate the saturation without compromising the initial luminance values. Sepia tones, which are the brownish tints commonly observed in vintage photographs, can be generated in conjunction with other single-color effects.
- You have complete control over the hues, including their vibrancy and saturation. To modify the chroma of an image, individual pixels must be relocated along the color wheel. Changing the red pixels to green, for instance, will cause the blue pixels to transition to green as well, and the yellow pixels to transform into cyan. By adjusting the saturation, the amount of gray in a color can be altered. The quantity of gray increases as the saturation value decreases. By adjusting the luminance, the chroma and saturation of the colors are altered.
- It is possible to substitute one or more hues. For instance, contemplate the substitution of every green hue for blue. Through the manipulation of these values, every color, including the initial ones, will transform.

- Fine-tune the image by manipulating the colors with low saturation while preserving the highly saturated pixels through the adjustment of the Vibrancy control. You will observe a general enhancement in the image's color saturation following the modifications, without the colors becoming excessively vibrant. Utilizing the Vibrancy control when increasing saturation in portraits can yield optimal outcomes by safeguarding skin tones and mitigating the potential for excessive saturation that can distort the subject's skin tone.

HOW TO CREATE A DUO-TONE IMAGE

The stages are as follows:

1. In the Adjust menu, navigate to Colorize, which follows Hue and Saturation. Follow these steps before utilizing the Colorize command to generate a duotone featuring nuanced color shifts: Navigate to **Image > Grayscale**, and from the resulting drop-down menu, select **Image > Increase Color Depth > RGB - 8 bits/channel.**
2. Input values or modify parameters via the following controls.
    - **Hue:** All existing colors can be modified by adjusting the hue.
    - **Saturation:** The saturation value is employed to modify the hue's intensity.

3. To continue, click the Okay button.

ADJUST THE LIGHTING, COLOR, AND SATURATION

Follow the following steps:

1. Select the desired option by selecting Adjust, then Hue and Saturation, and finally **Hue/Saturation/Lightness**. The Hue/Saturation/Lightness dialog pane is exhibited. The outermost color ring of the dialog box represents the color values in the initial condition of the image. The color ring in the center will be utilized to represent the altered values.

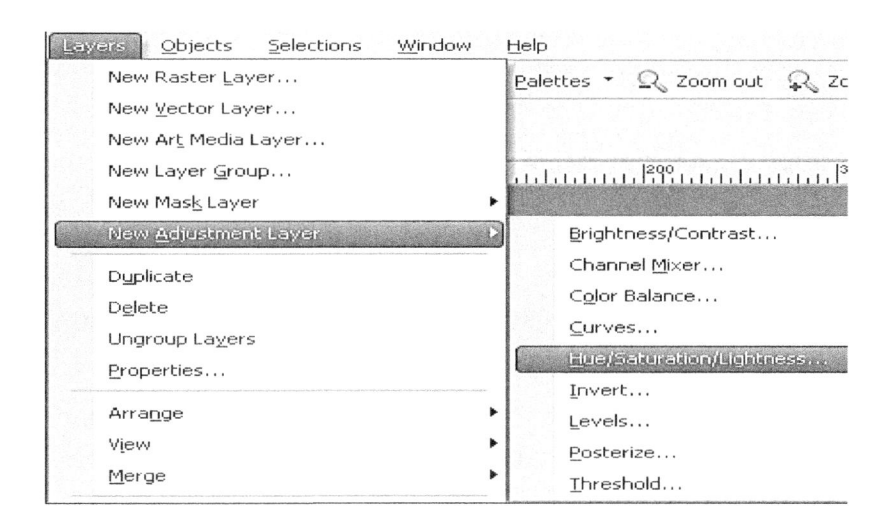

2. To proceed, choose an option from the Edit drop-down menu.

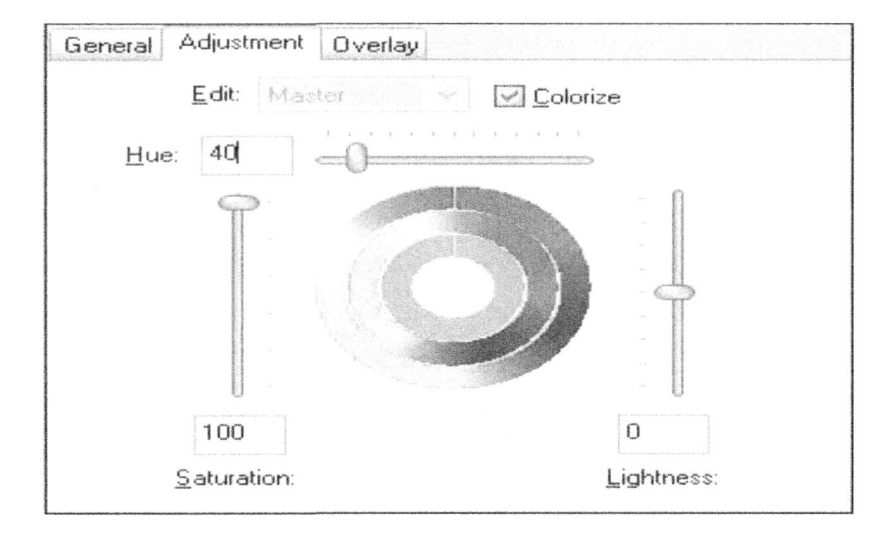

- Select the Master option to simultaneously modify all colors.

- To modify a particular color range, select one of the numerous. color alternatives from the drop-down menu.

In the process of editing a color range, the control ring situated between the inner and outer color rings can be employed to modify the specified range of colors. To modify the breadth of the range, manipulate the two periphery locations on the control ring. One can modify the range within which the adjustments will yield the most substantial impact by adjusting the two interior bars; the adjustments will be implemented between the bars. With the white circles, the adjustment area can be moved.

3. Modify the values on the Hue slider. The Hue value quantifies the extent to which the pixel's color has deviated from its initial state through the calculation of the number of complete rotations around the color wheel. When an object rotates in a clockwise direction, it is denoted by a positive value, whereas a negative value signifies inversion. As an illustration, when the Hue value is set to 180, blue transforms into yellow and green into magenta.
4. Pinch the Saturation slider until the desired level is achieved. Slide the slider in the desired direction—up to increase saturation, and down to decrease saturation. The value range is between -100 and 100. When this value is set to zero, the default configuration remains unaltered.
5. Modify the value of the toggle located beneath Lightness. To adjust the luminosity, one can do so by dragging the slider downwards, or by sliding the slider up. The value range is between -100 and 100. When this value is set to zero, the default configuration remains unaltered.
6. Navigate to the **OK icon**. By selecting the Colorize checkbox, the image will be converted to grayscale, resulting in the creation of a duotone or two-color image. Improve the visual representation through the process of hue selection, chroma adjustment, and luminance control.

Adjust the Colors

The stages are as follows:
1. Navigate to the Adjust menu, then select Hue and Saturation, then select the **Hue Map option**. The Hue Shift group box exhibits the altered colors in the bottom row of color boxes, whereas the upper row comprises the 10 original colors. Every color on the 360-degree color wheel corresponds to a distinct degree of rotation about the wheel.
2. Modify the corresponding color parameters when necessary.

3. Navigate to the **OK button**.

It could be taken one step further:

- The saturation levels of individual colors can be adjusted by typing a value within the range of −100 to 100 into the Saturation shift control.
- Manually alter the value or input a numerical value between -100 and 100 in the Lightness shift control to modify the darkness levels across all colors.

- To restore the colors to their initial configurations, select Default from the **Load Preset** drop-down menu.

HOW TO REMOVE AND ADJUST THE NOISE

"Noise" refers to the existence of extraneous pixel clusters or individual pixels within an image. There are numerous potential contributors to the cacophony. Camera malfunctions are frequently caused by faulty electrical components or file formats such as JPEG. The image exhibits various flecks of color, each of which represents disturbance. For a more distinct view of the disturbance, enlarge the image. Consider an azure expanse adorned with undertones of pink, red, green, and yellow.

In addition to providing a variety of options for removing different types of noise, PaintShop Pro also permits the addition of noise to an otherwise clear image.

By selecting either a specific area or the entire image, the following modifications can be made:

- Including a granular texture in an image can also diminish its level of detail. To optimize the visual appeal of an image, one should contemplate reducing the severity of minor imperfections and flaws that are not rectifiable through alternative editing applications. Merely introduce a modest quantity of disturbance into the image.

- By employing this methodology, one can readily discern and rectify minute blemishes that have a hue that deviates from the adjacent region.
- A prevalent issue in video capture photographs is the disparity in the capture rates of even and odd-numbered scan lines; this can be resolved. Probably, any motion of the subject at the time the image was taken would be discernible. Consider that removing scan lines can improve the visibility of the noise.
- It is possible to recover a JPEG image to its initial state. When any software program (such as scanning software) saves a file to the JPEG format, the data within the file is compressed to reduce its size. Several anomalies, including halos or color leakage, checkerboard patterns, and blocky regions, can result from compression. It is possible to remove undesirable patterns from scanned photographs. When reproduced on textured paper, digital photographs can be susceptible to this issue. To rectify the situation, eliminate single-pixel particles that consist primarily of black or white.
- Delete noise from an image while preserving border information through a process involving pixel luminance comparison with that of the adjacent pixels.
- It is possible to remove minuscule, distinct particles or regions of noise that are conspicuous among the remainder. Adjusting the intensity of each pixel to correspond with the median intensity of the adjacent pixels. The median intensity in the spectrum of potential intensities denotes the intermediate value as opposed to the mean. If you wish to maintain the object's boundaries, you can wish to employ the Median Filter function. You can fine-tune a pixel that distinguishes itself from its neighbors more effectively with this command than one that merges in. The number of adjacent pixels to be utilized in the computation can be specified. A greater pixel count will diminish noise, but it can result in the omission of some additional details.
- Multi-pixel black or white flecks, such as those resulting from dust accumulation on film or video, can be effectively eliminated by employing this methodology.

- Improve an image's quality by removing noise and particles while preserving the integrity of the original texture attributes. One potential strategy involves retaining the texture information present on an individual's garments while removing noise from another region of the image, say the face. In addition, the commands for One Step Noise Removal and Digital Noise Removal are available for use.

How to Add Noise

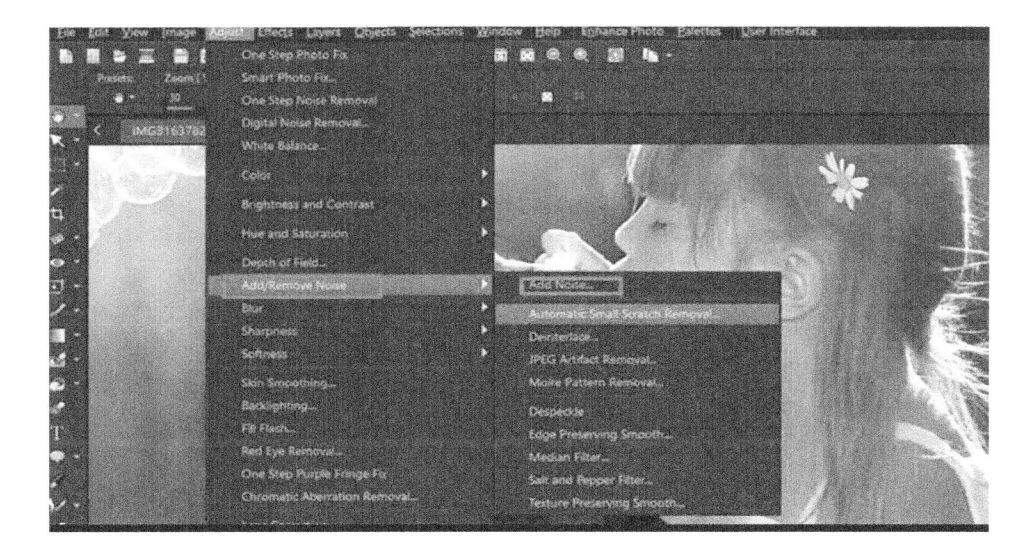

Apply noise using the instructions below in PaintShop Pro

1. From the **Adjust menu**, select the Add/Remove Noise option.
2. Select a noise pattern from the given options:
   - Generating a granular effect at random can improve the overall texture of an appearance.
   - Adjusts the color of the noise to match the original pixels uniformly.
   - In contrast to the Uniform option, the majority of noise appears more indistinguishable from the original pixels when the Gaussian option is utilized.
3. Determine the proportion of noise by selecting from the Noise drop-down menu or inputting a value into the Noise control.

4. Press the OK button. By checking the Monochrome option, black-and-white noise pixels can be utilized. Deactivate the checkbox to permit the utilization of colored pixels.

Removing more Weave Patterns

The stages are as follows:

1. Open the "**Adjust**" menu, navigate to "**Add/Remove Noise**," and then click "**Moire Pattern Removal**."
2. To optimize the image and increase the visibility of the complex patterns, modify the Zoom control by specifying a value or inputting one.
3. Modify the level of pattern eradication by selecting an option from the drop-down menu or inserting a value into the Fine details control. Individually modify the value by a small amount until the pattern is no longer visible. Select the minimum value that eliminates the pattern without significantly increasing it to achieve a clear image.
4. Modify the enlargement of the image by employing the zoom function within the dialog box. Proceed with this procedure until distinct color bands or blotches become apparent in the After pane. It is noteworthy that bands or blotches that are visible at 100% when the image is displayed can become more conspicuous as the level is decreased.
5. Gradually adjust the value of the Remove bands control until the visibility of color blotches or bands is diminished. To mitigate the risk of desaturation in tiny objects, employ the minimum value.
6. Press the OK button.

Following the effective elimination of the moire pattern, one can employ the Sharpness functions within the Adjust menu to reinstate intricacy and eradicate any remaining blurriness. However, this will not prevent the pattern from reappearing. To achieve optimal outcomes when utilizing the Sharpness commands and the Moire Pattern Removal dialog box, it is advisable to marginally increase the value of the Fine Details slider to an extent that suffices to eradicate the pattern.

Remove Individual Pixel Spots

Follow the following steps:

1. Determine the precise region within the image containing the particles and select it.

2. Select "**Adjust**," then "**Add/Remove Noise**," and lastly "**Despeckle**".

Removing Noise Distractions while Preserving the Image's Edges

The stages are as follows:

1. Determine the location of the disturbance that requires elimination, and subsequently select it.
2. Navigate to the "**Adjust**" menu, select "**Add/Remove Noise**," and select "**Edge Preserving Smooth**."
3. When modifying the "**Amount of smoothing**" parameter, either input an additional value or alter the current one. Choose the minimum blurring level that effectively removes particulates without compromising the integrity of the image's initial details. It is not possible to enter a value greater than 1.
4. Press the OK button. To achieve optimal outcomes, it is advisable to apply the Edge Preserving Smooth command exclusively to the problematic region of the image as opposed to utilizing it on the entire thing.

How to Remove Multi-pixel Specks

Follow the following steps:

1. Determine the location containing the particles and proceed with your selection.

2. Navigate to "**Add/Remove Noise**" > **Salt and Pepper Filter** from the "**Adjust**" menu.
3. Under the Speck size control or by selecting an item from the drop-down menu, it is possible to establish the minimum size, in pixels, of the largest speck that can be eliminated. Even numbers are never contained in this value.
4. Provide a value to the Sensitivity to speck control, indicating the minimum threshold of deviation necessary for an area to be categorized as a speck.
5. Press the OK button.

It is recommended to isolate the problematic area before implementing the Pepper Filter function on the complete image. By selecting the checkbox labeled "Include all lower speck sizes," specks that are smaller than the specified size value can be eliminated. To intensify the gravity of the reprimand, select the alternative labeled "Take aggressive action."

REMOVING DISTRACTIONS WHILE PRESERVING THE AUTHENTIC TEXTURES

The stages are as follows:

1. Determine the location of the unwanted noise and proceed with its selection.
2. Navigate to the "**Adjust**" navigation, select "**Add/Remove Noise**," and subsequently select "**Texture Preserving Smooth**."
3. Input a value into the Correction Amount control or select an option from the drop-down menu to make precise correction adjustments. A marginal reduction in noise is achieved by decreasing the value; the textured regions remain unaltered. While increasing the value effectively diminishes noise, it is possible that certain textured regions will not remain entirely intact.
4. Press the OK button.

CHOOSE A SPECIFIC AREA OF FOCUS

By outlining a selection around a region to capture an irregular shape, or by creating a circular or rectangular selection, you can quickly identify the focus area in PaintShop Pro . Additionally, an alternative can be inverted.

How to Adjust Blurred Areas

The blur applied to the region beyond the selection and the transition between the focused and blurred areas can be modified. Additionally, round or hexagonal aperture shapes are available for selection in Corel PaintShop Pro . The definition of light patterns in the obscured regions might be influenced by the aperture's configuration. Bokeh is the name given to this effect, which is most conspicuous when accompanied by dimly lit areas against a dark backdrop.

SET UP A FOCUS AREA USING THE FIELD OF DEPTH EFFECT

The stages are as follows:

1. Navigate to the Edit tab and select the area that requires emphasis.

2. Navigate to **Adjust > Depth of Field.**

3. Using the Blur slider, modify the degree of blur applied to the out-of-focus region.

You can:

- To invert the selected area, simply check the corresponding box labeled "Invert."
- Modify the effect of the transition from the area of focus to the area of blur.
- Modify the transition that occurs between the areas of focus and blurriness as necessary: Adjust the feather edge using the slider and

proceed accordingly. An increase in feathering is indicated by a rightward slider movement, whereas a decrease in feathering is indicated by a leftward slider movement. Notably, a value of zero will produce an undefined, jagged edge, which might not be the intended result. It is generally advisable to maintain this slider above 2 or 3.
- Modify the dimensions of the in-focus region by dragging the Focus range slider to the left to diminish the area in focus. Right-adjust the slider to emphasize the edge of the selected area.

In the Depth of Field dialog box, you can select a focus region using the Circular, Freehand, Rectangular, or Raster Selection tools if you have not yet done so. Make sure the selection is slightly larger than the area you wish to concentrate on, and then fine-tune the selection's edge using the Focus range slider.

HOW TO BLUR IMAGES

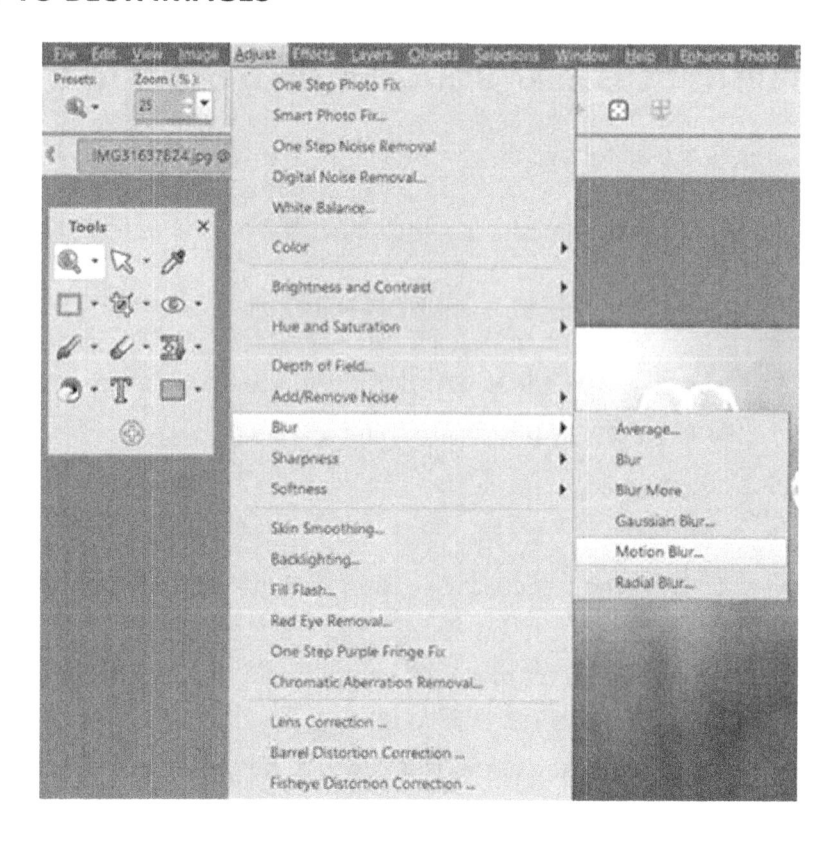

By utilizing the various commands provided by Corel PaintShop Pro , it is possible to distort your images.

Adjustments to a layer, a selection, or the entire image are as follows:
- One method of noise removal from an image involves modifying the luminance of each pixel to correspond with the mean brightness of its adjacent pixels. Additionally, the color dithering that occurs during the conversion of a paletted image to 24-bit color depth can be eliminated.
- To eliminate noise, reduce contrast, and create seamless transitions in your image.
- By employing a bell-shaped curve, a designated quantity of pixels should be blended gradually to modify the intensity of the blurring effect. The blurring is characterized by a smooth margin and a dense center.
- When photographing a moving subject, appropriately alter the exposure duration.

- It is possible to simulate the act of photographing a scene by manipulating the camera's speed or rapidly zooming in with a sluggish shutter speed.

Why would Someone Blur an Image?

One possible approach to improving a selection or image, repairing a photo, or reducing noise in an image is to utilize blurring commands. The Blur function produces smoother transitions and reduces contrast by calculating the mean of the pixels close to borders and regions characterized by substantial color variations. To augment the blurring effect, it is advisable to employ the Blur commands repetitively on the identical image.

HOW TO SHARPEN IMAGES

The uniformity introduced by digital cameras during the process of capturing images generally necessitates the application of sharpening the majority of the time. Sharpening can be necessary for images captured with digital cameras as opposed to film cameras, which are more susceptible to generating slightly out-of-focus images due to camera movement during capture. Generally, this issue is uncomplicated to resolve.

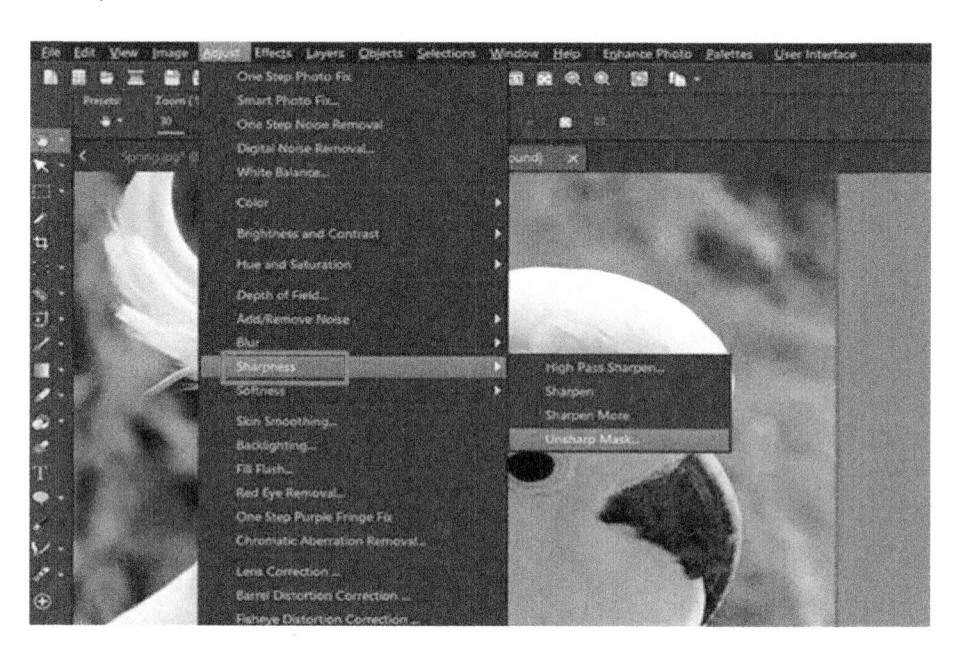

Before printing, sharing, or archiving, it is preferable to enhance your images so that they retain their quality regardless of color or tonal changes.

Enhancing commands in Corel PaintShop Pro can increase the contrast between adjacent pixels, thereby improving the quality of indistinct images. By applying the following commands, one can sharpen a selection, a layer, or the entire image:

- One should prioritize the improvement of high-frequency details, such as edges, while neglecting low-frequency components, including large structures, gradients, and background hues.
- Boost the contrast between adjacent pixels, specifically along the periphery of the image, to achieve a more distinct and transparent appearance.
- When we are talking about color correction, it is feasible to augment the contrast of an image's mid- to high-equilibrium margins while

preventing an escalation in noise. This technique is widely adopted by experts in the field.

Enhance the Level of Sharpness you Apply

Follow the following steps:

1. After selecting Sharpness from the Adjust menu, choose **High Pass Sharpen**.
2. Input a value between 0.00 and 250.00 to configure the radius at which pixels within a specified area are sharpened. It is important to note that images featuring close-up subjects and delicate details can necessitate higher Radius settings. Conversely, images containing an abundance of fine detail generally benefit from lower Radius settings.
3. To determine the overall intensity of the command, enter a value between 0 and 100 into the intensity control.
4. Select an option from the Blend mode drop-down menu to define how the high-frequency segments that have been sharpened will be incorporated into the original image.
    - **Hard Light:** In contrast to Overlay, it generates a greater degree of contrast, which deletes the neutral tones of the image and accentuates edge details.
    - **Soft Light:** Generates photographs that possess a delicate appearance.
5. Select OK.

How to use both low and high-frequency sharpening techniques

The stages are as follows:

1. Select **Unsharp Mask** from the menu labeled "**Adjust Sharpness**."
2. Input a radius (distance) between 0.01% and 100% in the Radius control to specify the region where pixels will be sharpened. It is important to

note that images featuring close-up subjects and delicate details can necessitate higher Radius settings. Conversely, images containing an abundance of fine detail generally benefit from lower Radius settings.
3. Enter a value between 1 and 500 into the intensity input to determine the overall intensity of the command.
4. The Clipping control accepts a value between 0 and 100 that specifies the minimum luminance values required for adjacent pixels to be sharpened.

5. Click the OK button.

SOFTEN IMAGES

A unique effect achieved with a high-quality soft-focus lens can be duplicated by applying a softening technique to a photograph; the result is a lustrous, dreamlike appearance. This aesthetic is frequently applied to magazine covers and glossy photographs.

By soft-focusing an image, a warmer appearance can be achieved. PaintShop Pro offers the following methods for softening:

- Apply a soft-focus camera lens effect to the selected image or input.

- If desired, a uniform, subtle haze can be applied to the entire image or a specific region.

WHAT OCCURS WITH PIXELS DURING IMAGE RESAMPLING?

When the Resize command is used to enlarge the dimensions of an image, it becomes necessary to interpolate additional pixels from the data already present in those pixels. Consider the following scenario: You possess a 100 by 100 pixel image and wish to enlarge it to 200 x 200 pixels. Scaling reduces an initial input of 10,000 pixels to 40,000 pixels in the final output. The remaining 75% of the pixels are essentially "created." It is common practice to fill in missing pixels through interpolation of the interpixel gaps that result from enlarging the image dimensions. The color of the adjacent pixel is replicated by employing the Pixel Resize method.

The Bilinear method calculates the mean value of four adjacent pixels within a 2x2 pixel neighborhood. The sophisticated Bicubic method employs sixteen adjacent pixels from a 4x4 pixel neighborhood. By augmenting the hues in the fictitious pixels, a more comprehensive understanding of the color transitions within that particular region of the image can be obtained as a result of the enlarged neighborhood.

To reduce the dimensions of an image, the Resize command calculates the average of its pixel colors. A picture is reduced from 100 by 100 pixels to 50 by 50 pixels.

With a total of 2,500 pixels, only a quarter of the pixels from the original image are displayed in the output. During averaging, the weight allocated to the original pixels is determined by the various resampling techniques employed.

ARE THERE ALTERNATIVE TECHNIQUES AVAILABLE FOR RESIZING IMAGES?

You can modify the dimensions of an image in many ways, including trimming it, editing the canvas size, publishing it in a different proportion, employing the Copy Special function, or utilizing the Save for Office function.

When the canvas size is increased, pixels are added to the image's edges. When the canvas size is decreased, pixels close to the image's boundaries become obscured, while the entire stratum of information remains intact. When an image is cropped, any pixels that extend beyond the designated region are removed.

By dragging the selection handles of an image you upload to the Print Layout box, you can resize it. This resizing method preserves the image file in its original state while publishing the image in a variety of dimensions.

The Copy Special command provides the ability to duplicate an image to the Clipboard in one of three sizes for various purposes, including professional printing, desktop printing, computer screen display, and email attachment. You can easily paste the resized image into a file in another application, such as a word processor, by transferring the image to the Clipboard.

In addition to enabling disk saving and image size and resolution adjustments, the Save for Office command offers comparable resizing capabilities to the Copy Special command.

HOW TO RESIZE IMAGES

The stages are as follows:

1. Select **Image > Resizing**.

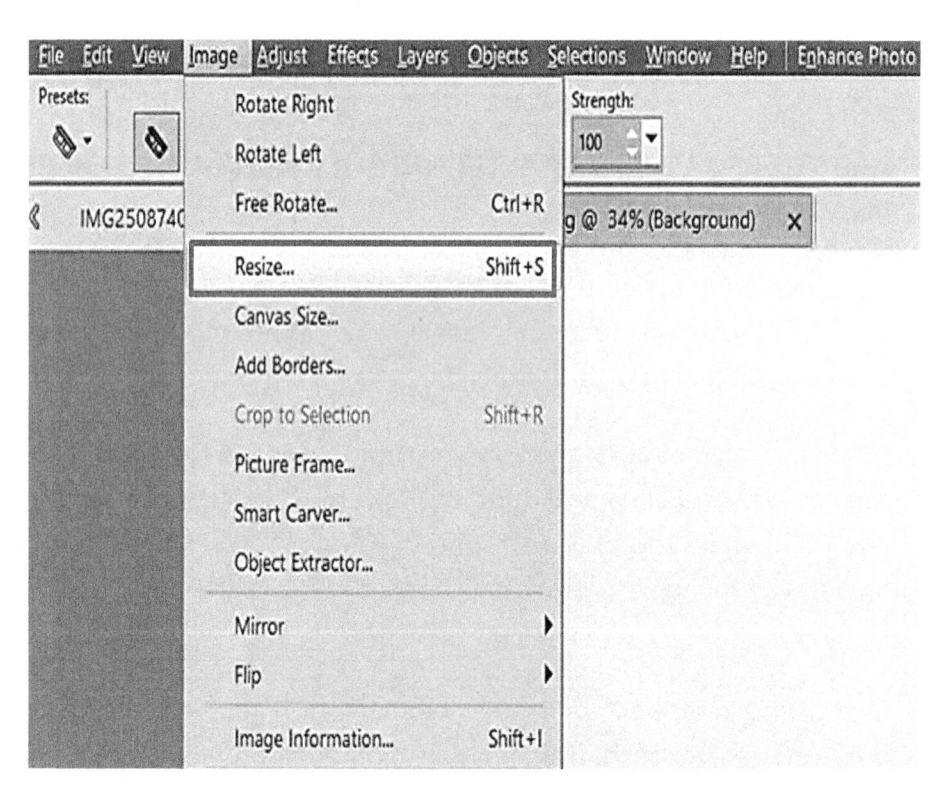

2. Select one of the following resizing options:

- When numerical values are entered into the Width and Height fields, the "By Pixels" alternative allows for the specification of the dimensions in pixels. A drop-down menu containing conventional measurements is an alternative option.
- To modify the dimensions, input a percentage value in the field labeled "Width" or "Height" (relative to the initial value).
- In the Print Size tab, enter values for width and height in inches, centimeters, or millimeters, respectively, to specify a size in those units. Additionally, the Resolution value can be modified, and a standard dimension can be selected via a drop-down menu.
- One-Sided Scaling—The image will be modified to reflect the present proportions. The user is provided with the choice to specify the width or height in pixels.

3. Select the Advanced and AI-Powered Settings checkbox and modify the options to achieve greater customization.

Moreover, you can additionally:

- **Pixel resampling**: The pixel dimensions of an image can be modified by adjusting the resolution setting while keeping the width and height parameters constant.
- **Sharpen the image after scaling:** To accomplish this, click "Use Resamples" and subsequently select "Bicubic" from the resulting drop-down menu. To resize an image, modify the Sharpness parameter to a value between 50 and 100. Notwithstanding the Sharpness control being configured to zero, the enlarged image retains its original level of sharpness.
- **Maintain the brightness of the image after resizing it:** In the General Program Preferences dialog box, under Miscellaneous options, select the Preserve picture brightness option to preserve the brightness of the image during resizing.

- **Unlock the aspect ratio:** To liberate the aspect ratio, remove the check from the Lock aspect ratio box.

- **Resize only the selected layer:** To perform a one-layer resizing, simply deselect the option labeled "resize all layers."

Adjustments to one control will affect the others if the Resample using checkbox is not selected; the Width, Height, and Resolution controls are interconnected in this manner. By utilizing this methodology, the pixel size of the image remains constant.

Image distortion will result from unequally extending or compressing the aspect ratio in different dimensions. A lock icon appears adjacent to the breadth and height input fields, signifying the locked state of the aspect ratio. You can preserve the current print size of the image by selecting the Maintain original print size checkbox.

USING UPSAMPLING POWERED BY AI TO MAKE YOUR IMAGES LARGER

When you expand (upsample) an image using the Resize box in Corel PaintShop Pro , AI-powered options become accessible. By analyzing image pixels, AI-powered solutions improve the clarity and level of detail in comparison to conventional upsampling techniques. In this situation, even low-resolution images can be useful. One potential solution is to have an older JPEG image captured using a low-quality camera or a cropped image that lacks the necessary resolution for printing.

It is critical to remember that the utilization of GPU acceleration has the potential to accelerate AI analysis. The optimal configuration should be determined through experimentation, as results can differ based on the configuration of your computer system. The maximum pixel size supported by AI-powered upsampling is 10,000 by 10,000 pixels. When the dimensions surpass this threshold, the option will become inactive.

INCREASING IMAGE SIZE THROUGH AI-POWERED UPSAMPLING

The stages are as follows:

1. Select an image, and then use the **Resize** option to modify its dimensions.
2. Select one of the following alternatives to enlarge the image:
    - When numerical values are entered into the Width and Height fields, the "By Pixels" alternative allows for the specification of the dimensions in pixels. A drop-down menu containing conventional measurements is an alternative option.
    - To modify the dimensions, input a percentage value in the field labeled "Width" or "Height" (relative to the initial value).
    - Under the By Print Size option, you can specify a dimension in millimeters, inches, or centimeters by entering values in the Width and Height boxes. Additionally, the Resolution value can be modified, and a standard dimension can be selected via a drop-down menu.
    - One-Sided Scaling—The image will be modified to reflect the present proportions. The user is provided with the choice to specify the width or height in pixels.
3. Ensure that the checkbox next to Advanced and AI-Powered Settings is checked.
4. Mark the "**AI-Powered**" checkbox next to "**Resample using**" and choose that option from the drop-down menu.
5. Select one of the following alternatives from the Mode tab:
    - **Photorealistic:** When capturing Images, select the photorealistic option.
    - **Illustration:** Select this alternative if you wish to incorporate drawings or additional illustrations.
6. The noise reduction intensity is selectable. To maintain more intricate pixel details, rotate the slider to the left; conversely, to attain more seamless margins, rotate the slider to the right.

7. Determining whether to activate or deactivate the GPU Acceleration option based on the specifications of your computer is essential.

8. After selecting OK, monitor the AI analysis's development by observing the green progress indicator situated at the program's bottom.

HOW TO WORK WITH COLORS AND MATERIALS

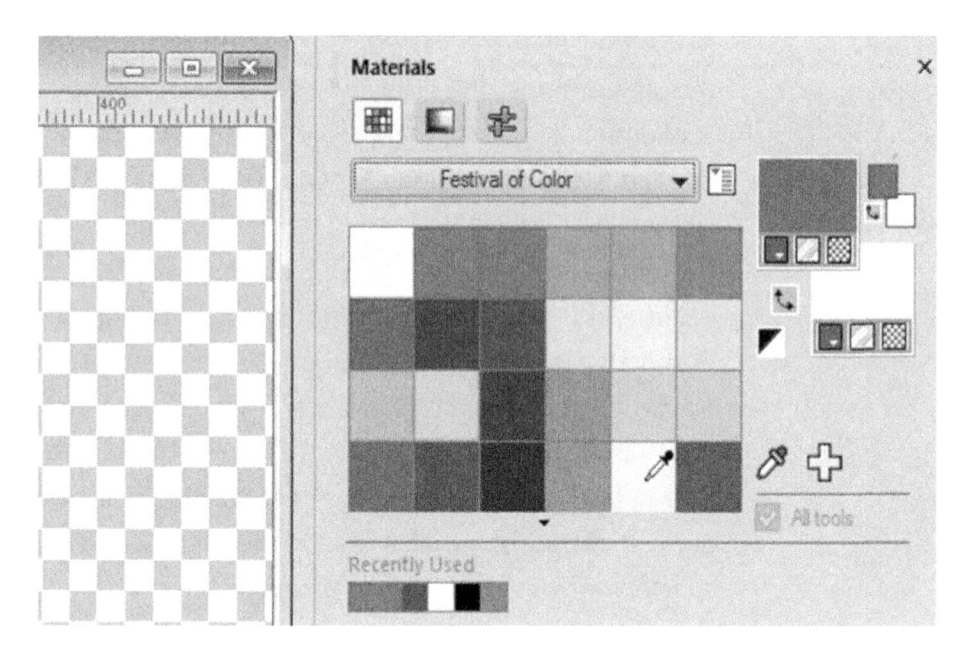

It is essential to have the ability to choose and manipulate colors and materials in Corel PaintShop Pro to perform tasks such as coloring images, designing scrapbook pages, and developing websites.

USING THE MATERIALS PALETTE IN PAINTSHOP ULTIMATE

You can paint, design, and fill with PaintShop Pro using an extensive variety of techniques and materials.

- The substance comprises a distinct design and, if desired, a texture.
- A style denotes a pattern, gradient, or color.

Utilizing the Materials pallet, one can select from an extensive variety of designs and materials. At all times, the Materials pallet is readily accessible. You can choose to maintain its visibility while working, or only reveal it when necessary. Consider inverting the hues or materials of the foreground and background.

SELECT COLORS FROM THE DESKTOP OR AN IMAGE

You can choose a foreground or background color from an open image or a color in the interface while working in PaintShop Pro. Utilizing this feature can be highly beneficial when one requires color coordination with the Windows desktop or the hue of a particular icon. Additionally, users are presented with the opportunity to choose a color from a variety of programs or websites listed in a web browser.

To utilize a sampled color from one image as a fill for another region or image, the Sample and Fill mode can be enabled.

Using the Eyedropper Tool allows you to Select Colors from the Image you are Currently Working on

The stages are as follows:

1. Select the Dropper application from the Tools menu.
2. As shown below, configure the settings on the Tool Options panel:
   - Select the desired sample size in pixels from the drop-down menu.
   - Ensure that the checkbox labeled "Sample from all image layers" is selected.
3. Utilize the left mouse button to select the image as the foreground or background color.

To modify the background color or to select a foreground color, right-click the image while holding down **Ctrl**. By following this method, it is also possible to choose a hue from the image while utilizing brush tools, including the Eraser and paintbrush.

USE THE DROPPER TOOL TO SELECT COLORS AND FILL AND SAMPLE ACCORDINGLY

The stages are as follows:

1. Select the **Dropper tool** from the Tools menu.
2. Select the **Sample and Fill option** from the Options panel of the tool.
3. The desired color for experimentation can be selected from the picture display. Upon selection, the tool icon immediately transforms into a filled icon.
4. By selecting the area you wish to fill with the sampled color, you can select it. The dispersal and interaction of the fill with the backdrop are determined by the final parameters of the Flood Fill tool.

Select your Colors from the Desktop

The stages are as follows:

1. Ensure that the desired color is visible on the screen.
2. Select the **Sample Color option** from the dialog pane labeled Materials.
3. Move the cursor over the desired-colored portion of the desktop. Websites and open windows of any kind are encompassed within this classification.
4. Select the tab in which the sampled area must be filled in. As one hovers over regions that are amenable to sampling, the Sample Color pipette icon will manifest.

CHAPTER EIGHT

GRADIENT AND PATTERNS

USING GRADIENTS

The blending of two or more hues produces a gradient. By applying gradients to areas to be filled in, painted, or drawn, one can generate captivating effects or seamless color transitions. Gradients can be used to create a shiny or glowing effect, add dimension to elements, and design web buttons with shadows and accents. Implementing a black-to-white gradient to conceal and seamlessly integrate visual elements of a website with other content.

HOW TO APPLY YOUR CURRENT GRADIENT

Select the appropriate property box from the Style drop-down menu, either the **Foreground and Stroke Properties box** or the **Background and Fill Properties box**, from the Materials palette. Subsequently, click the Gradient icon. The gradient that was most recently chosen will be implemented.

How to Save Edited Gradients

Follow the following steps:

- Choose Save. Remember to select Save at all times on the Gradient page.

- After delineating the name for the gradient, select OK.

How to Create Gradients

1. Click the **New Gradient icon** located on the Gradient page to commence.

2. After giving the new gradient a name, click OK. The gradient is generated by positioning two markers, each carrying a unique color, at 0% and 100%.

Change the Names of Gradients

The stages are as follows:

1. To access the Resource Manager, navigate to the Gradient page and click the **More Options icon.**
2. Select the desired renamed gradient via its click in the Resource Manager dialog box.
3. Click OK after entering a name in the Rename Resource dialog box.

Remove Gradients

Follow the following steps:

1. Select a gradient from the newly created Gradient page.
2. Select "**Delete Gradient**" from the resulting menu.
3. Select "**Yes**" to validate the deletion.

Editing Gradients

The transparency, colors, and transition points of gradients are all customizable. Alternatively, you can generate your gradients or modify preset ones. It is possible to save, remove, or rename gradients.

Midpoints and markers within the Gradient Editor serve to indicate the transparency, transition points, and hues of a gradient.

- **Markers:** The gradient bar exhibits transparency indicators positioned at its uppermost tab. Indicators of color are discernible beneath the gradient bar.

- **Midpoints:** These points denote the equilibrium of color blend between two hues or the 50% opacity level. A midpoint is situated in the space between every pair of markers.

It is simple to insert, eliminate, modify the transparency of, alter the color of, and relocate markers. Remember that any modifications you make to the default gradient are irrevocably preserved. To maintain the integrity of the initial gradients, ensure that any modifications are stored in a fresh gradient file.

ADJUSTING THE MIDPOINTS OR MARKERS

Modify the position of the midpoint or marker within the Gradient Editor. Additionally, you can enter a value in the Location field either before or after selecting the marker with a click.

How to Add Markers

To incorporate markers, navigate to the Gradient Editor and select the desired option (above the gradient bar for a transparency marker or beneath the gradient bar for a color marker). The hue of the highlighted gradient bar is applied to the marker, regardless of whether it is Fore, Back, or Custom.

Changing the Color of a Marker

The stages are as follows:

1. By selecting beneath the gradient bar, a marker can be selected in the Gradient Editor. The upper triangle of the marker changes color from white to black.
2. Once you have finished one of the following duties, **click OK:**
    - Select "**Fore**" to utilize the hue of the foreground from the menu. Remember to select the background color by clicking the Back icon.

- **When choosing a new custom color:** select a color from the color page by selecting the swatch adjacent to the user icon.

- To select a color directly from the gradient itself, select the gradient bar.

The hues of the gradient that is applied will be dynamic when the foreground and background colors are combined. By applying custom colors from the User palette to each marker, a uniform gradient can be achieved in contrast to static colors.

Adjusting the Midpoints or Markers

The stages are as follows:

1. To make a selection, select the marker located above the gradient bar in the gradient editor.
2. Controlling opacity requires the entry or modification of a value. The values for complete transparency span a range of 0% to 100%. Opaque in color. At 100%, the particles are entirely concealed.

ADJUST GRADIENTS ON VECTOR OBJECTS AND INSTANTLY SEE THE CHANGES

The stages are as follows:

1. After selecting the **Pick tool** from the Tools toolbar, a gradient-containing vector object should be selected in the image window.
2. In the Materials panel, select the **Background and Fill Properties swatch** to open the Material Properties dialog box.
3. To modify the gradient parameters, navigate to the Gradient pane.

Exporting and Importing Gradients

After developing a new gradient, contemplate exporting it for use in another application. The GRD file format, which is widely implemented across multiple applications, is utilized to hold the default gradients. GRD files also support the importation of gradients.

Exporting Gradients

To export the desired gradient from the Gradient page, follow these steps:

1. Locate and select the gradient from the gradient page that you wish to export.
2. Select **Export** from the menu labeled More Options.
3. Select a location for the gradient to be saved. Within the Gradients folder of the PaintShop Pro software, you will find the default gradients.
4. Input the name of the newly created gradient in the field labeled "**File name**."

5. Navigate to Save.

How to Import GRD Gradients

The stages are as follows:

1. From the **More Options menu** on the Gradient page, select Import.
2. Proceed to the directory containing the gradient you wish to use. The folder comprises an exhaustive enumeration of all GRD files.

3. After selecting the filename of the gradient, click Open.

USING PATTERNS

Inspire your imagination through painting, drawing, or color-filling patterns. PaintShop Pro provides its users with an extensive assortment of templates, encompassing various aesthetic choices such as stained glass, zebra patterns, and brickwork. Patterns can be generated by utilizing an image or a specific segment thereof.

Patterns impart a distinctive element to the visuals that one has produced. Patterned text, objects featuring patterned inserts or borders, and patterned brush strokes are all achievable. Produce tiled graphics for stationery, websites, and paper products. To design visually enticing backgrounds for a variety of projects, including CD covers, calendars, and greeting cards, patterns are indispensable. Patterns are readily available online without any associated cost.

HOW TO SELECT PATTERNS

The stages are as follows:

1. Choose one of the options listed below from the Materials panel:
   - To select a foreground pattern from the available options, click the Foreground and Stroke Properties box.
   - To choose a background pattern from the available options, click the Background and Fill Properties box.
2. Select the preferred pattern.
3. On the Design page, click the thumbnail of the pattern you wish to utilize.
4. As required, modify the following controls:
   - Indicating the pattern's direction, the angle value can vary between 0 and 359 degrees.
   - The scale value is employed to denote the true magnitude of the image, which can range from 10 to 250. A decrease in value corresponds to an increased probability that the image will recur numerous times within the pattern. An increase in value can result in the possibility that the image will be cropped or lose detail, causing it to appear hazy.
5. Navigate to the OK icon.

How to use a Selection or an Active Image as a Pattern

The stages are as follows:

1. Launch the desired image you want to use.

2. Choose an area of the image to transform into the pattern. The Material Properties dialog box provides access to the thumbnail representation of the pattern as it appears on the Pattern tab.

USING TEXTURES

To accomplish the appearance of textured paper or canvas, one can paint, draw, or incorporate a texture. Textures can be combined with various hues, gradients, or patterns to generate fills and strokes for the foreground and background. PaintShop Pro offers an extensive collection of textures, such as aged paper, fractured pavement, and clouds. Custom textures can be generated by starting with an existing image.

Apply Current Texture

To apply the currently selected texture, proceed by clicking the **Texture icon** located in either the Foreground and Stroke Properties box or the Background and Fill Properties box on the Materials interface. Verify that the recently selected texture is currently active.

How to Select a Texture

1. Choose one of the following actions to execute from the Materials palette:
    - To select a foreground texture from the available options, click the Foreground and Stroke Properties box.

- To choose a background texture from the available options, click the Background and Fill Properties box. Anticipate the appearance of the Material Properties dialog box.
2. Select the desired texture.
3. Ensure that the "**Add Texture**" checkbox is checked on the page where the texture will be displayed.
4. To select a texture, simply click on its preview image.
5. Modify the texture by applying the requisite adjustments to the following controls:
    - The value indicates the texture's angle (or orientation) and ranges from 0 to 359 degrees.
    - Scale denotes the actual magnitude of the image, which can differ between 10 and 250. A decrease in value increases the probability that the image will appear multiple times on the texture. Elevating the value might lead to the cropping of the image, a reduction in detail, or the introduction of blurriness.

As you modify the parameters, the generated content, including the texture and design, will be displayed in the Current preview box.

6. Navigate to the **OK icon**.

You have the option to do the following:

- Modify the content's presentation: It is imperative to refine the configurations after selecting the Color, Gradient, or Pattern buttons.

- Employ the most recent resources for each instrument. Select the "All tools" checkbox adjacent to it on the Materials panel. Deselecting the checkbox will restrict the impact of the materials in use to the active tool exclusively.

It is still possible to incorporate a variety of fillings and strokes to progressively deepen and fill in the texture. Multiple applications of fillings or strokes are required to attain the desired outcome. By navigating the control needle within the texture preview on the Pattern page, it is possible to modify the texture's angle. Presenting one of the alternatives at your disposal.

HOW TO SAVE PHOTOS AS TEXTURES

The stages are as follows:

1. Produce an image utilizing PaintShop Pro or an analogous application.
2. Save the image as a BMP file in either the Textures folder of the PaintShop Pro application or the Documents/Corel PaintShop Pro/ folder. A thumbnail of the texture can be accessed via the Material Properties dialog box, specifically by navigating to the Texture page and selecting the Texture heading. Each file contained within the Textures folder of the PaintShop Pro application folder is represented visually as thumbnails within the texture thumbnails tab.
3. Change the default storage location of the texture files by selecting **File Location** from the drop-down menu that appears after selecting the **More Options option**.

USING SWATCHES AND CUSTOM COLOR PALETTES

A swatch that is saved will be incorporated into a customized palette. Create an unlimited number of palettes. An illustration of this is the application of a customized pallet to arrange every color and material associated with a particular undertaking. Palette contents that are no longer required can be removed.

A custom color palette developed in PaintShop Pro can now be imported. As an illustration, an organization might collaborate on the application of its corporate hues by utilizing a palette comprising custom swatches.

Swatches

Combining and storing combinations of colors, gradients, patterns, or textures constitutes the creation of a sampler. Color samples Swatches facilitate the recall of preferred color combinations, design styles, and material varieties when working on projects.

Selecting samples is possible, along with creating, modifying, removing, and renaming them. You are granted the ability to alter how swatches are presented. The location of the swatch files (.pspscript) is identical to that of the palette folder. Folders are used to contain palettes. In the absence of modifying the default location, you might discover the patches in the [C] folder. Corel PaintShop Pro documents for user [user name].

Select Color Palettes

Proceed by following these steps:

1. In the Materials panel, select the **Swatches tab** and then click its icon.

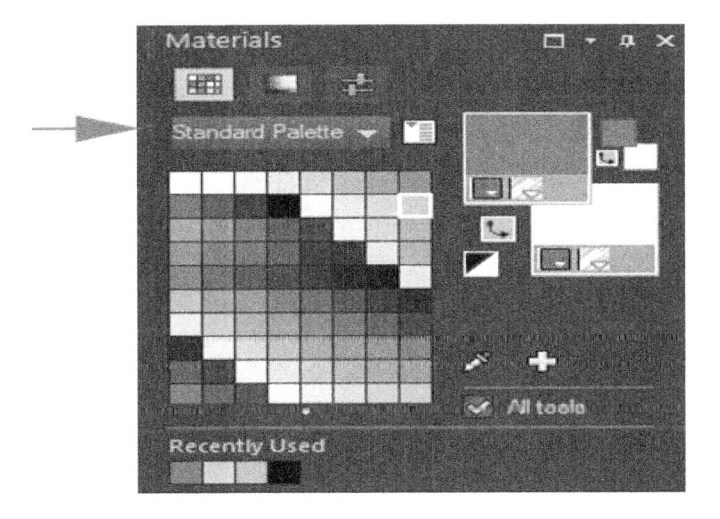

2. When you select the Palette menu, a drop-down menu will appear from which you can select a color palette.

Creating Palettes

The procedures:

1. Select and select the **Swatches tab** within the Materials panel.
2. Select the New Palette option that appears after clicking More Options.
3. After providing a name for your palette, click OK to continue. The palette is accessible via the drop-down menu located immediately above the samples. Swatches are now an option that can be incorporated into a palette. By convention, the color scheme is saved in the [C:] folder by default.

How to Import a Swatch Palette

To continue, select one of the following alternatives:

- Transfer the folder containing the palette and. pspscript files for every swatch to the location designated by the default user. The directory containing the file/swatches is C: Users[user name]DocumentsCorel PaintShop Pro.

- Transfer the palette folder, which comprises the pspscript files corresponding to every swatch in the palette, to a desired destination. Then, click Add after navigating to the location where the palette folder was saved by selecting File > Preferences > File Locations, then Swatches in the File types list.

Create Swatches

To access the Swatches tab within the Materials interface, proceed as follows: click on its icon.

1. Select the **Swatches tab** from the panel labeled Materials.
2. Select the desired hue, and then select the button labeled "**Add to Palette**."

3. Click OK after selecting a palette from the Add to Palette dialog box. An alternative approach is to utilize the New icon to produce a fresh pallet.
4. Input the swatch's name into the New Swatch dialogue pane. The name of a sample in the Materials palette is displayed in the tooltip when the cursor is hovered over it.
5. Select the **"OK"** option. Bear in mind that to access the Materials panel, you can select New Swatch from the drop-down menu accessible by clicking the More Options icon.

Selecting a Swatch

The stages are as follows:

1. Select the icon associated with the Swatches tab in the Materials interface.
2. Required: One of the following options
    - To continue, select the fragment that will serve as the material for the foreground.
    - One can choose a swatch as the background material by performing a right-click.

Renaming Swatches

The stages are as follows:

1. Select and select the Swatches tab within the Materials panel.
2. Select the desired swatch for renaming by clicking on it.
3. After selecting the **More Options icon**, from the resulting drop-down menu, select Rename Swatch.

Changing the Display of Swatches

After accessing the Materials palette, navigate to the Swatches menu and utilize the following options:

- **Select the swatch types to display:** To exhibit a specific category of swatches, select **View** from the drop-down menu that appears after clicking the **More Options icon**.
- **Change the order in which the swatches are sorted:** To arrange items according to name or style, select the Sort By option from the menu that appears when you click the More Options icon. By default, the samples will be arranged in this particular configuration consistently.

- **Change the sizes of the swatch thumbnails:** To modify the dimensions of the swatch thumbnails, select Small, Medium, or Large Thumbnails from the drop-down menu after selecting the "**More Options**" icon. By default, thumbnails of a medium size will be displayed.

CHAPTER NINE

TIPS, TRICKS AND TROUBLESHOOTING

TIPS AND TRICKS

Corel PaintShop Pro is a versatile and potent image editing application. It is utilized for a multitude of purposes, including the creation of digital artwork, the modification of images, and the development of graphic designs, by both experts and novices. Having the knowledge and understanding of the hints and techniques can significantly increase your efficiency and lead to superior results, irrespective of your level of expertise as a user.

In the following discussion, we shall expound upon an exhaustive assemblage of strategies and recommendations that shall optimize your utilization of Corel PaintShop Pro , fostering both efficiency and innovation.

CUSTOMIZE YOUR WORKSPACE

One can achieve a substantial increase in productivity by customizing their workspace to align with their individual preferences. By utilizing the numerous customization options available in Corel PaintShop Pro, you can arrange the software's panels, toolbars, and menus in the most practical fashion for your workflow. An individual's distinct work environment can be archived for future convenience.

To customize one's working environment:

1. To access the workspace, select "**Workspace**" from the "**Window**" menu.
2. To modify the arrangement of menus, toolbars, and panels, navigate to the "**Customize Workspace**" menu.
3. To improve accessibility, resize panels, transfer them to other positions, or combine them.

4. To preserve the customized workspace, choose "**Save As**" and provide a name for the folder before clicking "**Save**."

USE SHORTCUTS ON THE KEYBOARD

To enhance efficiency and accomplish tasks more quickly, the utilization of keyboard shortcuts is an absolute necessity. By providing an extensive library of keyboard shortcuts for a variety of operations, Corel PaintShop Pro enables users to access tools and features efficiently, minimizing any interruptions to their creative process.

Among the numerous useful keyboard shortcuts are:

- **Ctrl + Z**: Undo
- **Ctrl + Shift + Z:** Copy and Paste
- To redo, press and hold the **C key**.
- **Ctrl + D**: Deselect
- **Ctrl: T:** Transform
- **Ctrl + A:** Select All

Furthermore, it is possible to customize keyboard shortcuts to align with individual preferences through the following path: "**File**" > "**Preferences**" > "**Customize**" > "**Keyboard Shortcuts**."

MASTER SELECTION TOOLS

To selectively modify or isolate specific areas of an image for editing, selection tools are indispensable. A diverse array of selection tools is accessible within Corel PaintShop Pro, with each tool specifically engineered to perform a particular purpose. Abilities for editing will be substantially enhanced if these tools are mastered.

Frequent examples of selection techniques include the following:

- **Marquee selection tool**: The marquee selection tool enables the user to make decisions that are elliptical in shape or rectangular in shape.
- **Magic Wand Tool:** Employ the Magic Wand Tool to select regions that share a comparable hue or tone.
- **Freehand selection tool:** The Freehand Selection Tool is an application that allows users to generate choices through the use of freehand sketches.
- **Selection Brush tool:** The Selection Brush Tool enables the user to apply selections to an image.

To determine which selection tool best fulfills your editing needs, you should experiment with many different tools. Additionally, you can enhance your decisions by employing tools like "**Feather**" and "**Refine Edge**" to accomplish more seamless transitions.

CHECK OUR ADJUSTMENT LAYERS

By employing adjustment layers, which function as non-destructive editing tools, it is possible to apply alterations to images while preserving the original captured pixel data. This capability is granted to you by the ability to experiment with modifications and simply revert to the original image when necessary.

If you want to add a layer for adjustment:

- To generate a fresh adjustment layer, navigate to the "**Layers**" menu and choose the "**New Adjustment Layer**" option.
- A variety of options are available for adjusting brightness and contrast, levels, curves, hue and saturation, and additional attributes of the image.
- To achieve the intended outcome, modify the parameters of the adjustment layer as required.

Adjustment layers enable users to selectively modify elements, mask off specific regions, and fine-tune modifications at any given time.

ACQUIRE KNOWLEDGE OF LAYER MASKING TECHNIQUES

By employing layer masking, it is possible to expose or conceal portions of a layer without losing pixel data permanently. This is achieved by either concealing or exposing the stratum. Various applications can significantly benefit from this, including the blending of photographs, the creation of composites, and the implementation of selective adjustments.

The following describes how to create a layer mask:

1. Select the specific layer to which the mask is to be applied.
2. Click the "**Add Layer Mask**" icon situated in the Layers panel's bottom-right corner.
3. When applying a layer mask, one can utilize brushes or selection tools to apply black paint for concealment purposes, or white paint to expose any subject matter.

To achieve seamless blending across multiple layers, it is advisable to conduct experiments utilizing a range of brush sizes, opacities, and blending modes. Furthermore, gradient masks can be employed to establish smooth transitions between distinct segments.

USE SMART SELECTION TOOLS

To autonomously identify and select regions or objects within an image according to their color, tone, or texture, intelligent selection tools employ complex algorithms. While confronted with challenging decisions, these instruments have the potential to streamline the process and save time.

Corel PaintShop Pro includes the following sophisticated selection capabilities:

- **Smart Selection Brush:** Employs the Smart Selection Brush to autonomously select items that share similar hues and textures.
- **Smart Edge:** A feature known as "Smart Edge" refines selection edges to enable more precise masking.
- **Smart Selection Tool:** Item selection is automated via the Smart Selection tool, which considers the color and tone of the product.

It is advisable to experiment with these tools and optimize their sensitivity settings to achieve optimal outcomes for the images under consideration.

USE TEMPLATES AND PRESETS THAT ARE AVAILABLE

The utilization of presets and templates can facilitate the streamlining of one's workload by offering pre-established configurations and layouts for frequently executed operations. Corel PaintShop Pro offers an extensive collection of presets and templates that can be utilized for a variety of purposes, including the creation of social media posts, visual effects for images, and graphic designs.

Explore the preset manager, where you can search for and implement presets comprising brushes, gradients, effects, and other elements. Furthermore, it is possible to create and save personalized presets for future use.

You can utilize previously created layouts that have been made available to you as templates as a foundation for your endeavors. Implementing templates can be a beneficial way to initiate the creative process, regardless of whether you are producing a social media graphic, greeting card, or collage.

TRY OUT DIFFERENT FILTERS AND EFFECTS

Filters and effects constitute a potent method for embellishing and customizing your photographs. Corel PaintShop Pro offers its users an extensive assortment of filters and effects, encompassing artistic filters, photographic effects, and various types of text effects.

Explore an assortment of filters and effects to imbue your photographs with a sense of uniqueness and ingenuity. The following instances illustrate well-liked filters and effects:

- **Gaussian Blur:** By flattening images, the application of Gaussian Blur generates a dreamlike effect.
- **Sharpen:** This mode improves the image's clarity and detail by applying a sharpening effect.
- **Sepia:** The sepia effect imparts an aged appearance to images by imparting a sepia tone.
- **Vignette:** To draw attention to the center of an image, the vignette is a technique in which the borders of the image are darkened.

Utilize an assortment of filters and effects to endow your photographs with an appearance that is singular and unique.

USE PLUGINS TO ACCESS ADDITIONAL FUNCTIONALITY

Modules, which are frequently referred to as plugins, are extensions created by external developers to augment the functionality of Corel PaintShop Pro. To fulfill specific needs such as enhancing workflow capabilities, obtaining distinctive effects, or gaining access to sophisticated retouching tools, modules can expand the program's capabilities.

Examples of prevalent plugins for Corel PaintShop Pro include the following:

- Nik Collection is an assortment of imaginative filters and effects that provide an extensive range of choices.
- Topaz Labs is an organization that provides advanced tools for the enhancement and processing of images.

- One can attain a vintage aesthetic by employing Alien Skin Exposure, which stimulates film textures and effects.

A marketplace for plugins can contain applications that enhance one's creative capabilities and integrate with one's workflow, which can be discovered and installed.

ENGAGE IN NON-DESTRUCTIVE EDITING

By employing non-destructive editing techniques, it is possible to modify images without causing any lasting damage to the pixel data that was initially captured. As a result, it is possible to conduct experiments and make adjustments without compromising the image's quality at any given time. **To practice editing without causing damage:**

- It is advisable to employ alteration layers instead of conducting simple modifications to the images.
- One should target particular layers or objects with modifications rather than implementing them on the entire image.

- To preserve the ability to make changes to your work, you must save it in a layered file format, such as PSPIMAGE or PSD.

By employing non-destructive editing techniques, one can exert greater control over modifications and easily revert to previous stages when necessary.

TROUBLESHOOTING PAINTSHOP PRO

Users of the comprehensive image editing program Corel PaintShop Pro have access to a vast array of tools and functionalities for enhancing and modifying images. Nevertheless, similar to any other software application, it can encounter occasional issues. The objective of this troubleshooting guide is to offer clients additional support in resolving common challenges that can arise while utilizing Corel PaintShop Pro .

SYSTEM REQUIREMENTS

To ascertain the compatibility of your computer with Corel PaintShop Pro , it is critical to verify that it meets the bare minimum requirements before commencing troubleshooting.

TYPICAL PROBLEMS AND POSSIBLE SOLUTIONS

Performance Problems

The efficacy of the Corel PaintShop Pro software is subpar or experiencing delays.
Possible resolution:

- Ensure that your personal computer meets the mandatory minimum system requirements.
- Delete any non-essential secondary applications to free up system resources.
- Update the drivers associated with your graphics card to the latest available version.
- To enhance the efficacy of the image under consideration, decrease its dimensions or optimize it.
- Deactivate any modules or features that are not in use and do not need to be present.
- Should the performance issues persist, you might consider upgrading your equipment.

Freezing or Crashing

Corel PaintShop Pro frequently freezes or crashes, constituting an issue that requires attention.

Possible solution:

- Ensure that the software is currently installed and up-to-date. After confirming that updates are available, proceed with their installation.
- Temporarily disabling third-party plugins or extensions will allow you to identify whether they are the root cause of the issue.
- Modify Corel PaintShop Pro to restore it to its initial configuration. This option is frequently accessible through the menu containing the preferences or settings.
- Employ the software for administrative purposes. Select the PaintShop Pro shortcut using the right mouse button, and then click "**Run as administrator**."
- Should the issues persist, it would be advisable to attempt a fresh installation of Corel PaintShop Pro or contact Corel support for further assistance.

Brush or Tool Problems

Regarding utensils and instruments, their proper operation is being compromised.

Possible difficulty:

- I would like to emphasize the importance of selecting the proper brush or implement for the task at hand.
- Verify that the brush parameters have been accurately specified through a check. Considerations such as the parameters for size, opacity, and hardness are crucial.
- If one suspects inadvertent modification of the tool or brush settings, it is advisable to revert them to their initial configuration.
- One potential solution is to restart Corel PaintShop Pro to observe whether the issue resolves itself.

- If the problem persists, you might consider reinstalling the application or contacting Corel support for assistance.

Problems with the Workspace or the Interface

The workspace or interface of Corel PaintShop Pro exhibits indications of deformation or layout complications.

Possible solution:

- Ensure that the default configuration of the workspace has been restored. This option is frequently accessible through the menu containing the preferences or settings.
- You must modify the display parameters of your monitor to verify that Corel PaintShop Pro is compatible with them.
- Update the drivers associated with your graphics card to the latest available version.
- If you are utilizing a multitude of monitors, attempt to diagnose the issue by disconnecting one of them to determine if the problem is caused by the display's configuration.
- Should the problem persist, you have the option of reinstalling Corel PaintShop Pro or contacting Corel support for further assistance.

Issues with the File Compatibility

The issue is that certain file formats cannot be opened or saved in Corel PaintShop Pro .

Possible Solution:

- It is imperative to verify whether the file format being attempted to access or save is compatible with Corel PaintShop Pro. A compilation of the supported file formats can be obtained by consulting the program's documentation.
- It is your responsibility to ascertain whether the file you are trying to access is corrupt. You could verify this by launching the image in an alternative image editing application.

- It is advisable to upgrade to the latest version of Corel PaintShop Pro, as newly released updates frequently include support for additional file formats.
- It is recommended to convert the file to an alternative format using an independent software application before attempting to access it in Corel PaintShop Pro.
- If you continue to encounter issues with file compatibility, please contact Corel support for further assistance.

Activation or Licensing Document Difficulties

An issue has been identified with the license or activation of Corel PaintShop Pro .

Possible Solution:
- You are responsible for verifying the validity of the license key or activation code you supply. Perform a thorough review to identify any typographical or error entries that may have been introduced.
- To proceed with activation, you must guarantee that your internet connection is operational and consistent.
- Before reinstalling Corel PaintShop Pro on the same computer, ensure that the program has been completely uninstalled from any other installations.
- For further assistance, please contact Corel support if you encounter challenges related to your license or activation.

Problems with the Printing Process

The issue is that Corel PaintShop Pro is encountering complications during the process of transferring images to the printer or fails to produce accurate prints.

Possible Solution:
- Ensure that the printer's driver software is current. You can obtain and subsequently install the most recent drivers by downloading them from the manufacturer's website.

- Verify that the print parameters are appropriately configured in Corel PaintShop Pro by conducting a thorough inspection of them. Various parameters warrant cautious consideration, such as print quality, paper size, and orientation.
- Confirm that the printer is powered on and that the connection between it and the computer is accurate.
- Before you begin publishing, you must ensure that the network printer you are utilizing is operational and accessible.
- To ascertain whether the problem is specific to Corel PaintShop Pro, attempt to reproduce the image using an alternative program; if the issue persists, proceed accordingly.

Management Color Issues

The color representation in Corel PaintShop Pro appears inaccurate or diverges from that observed on alternative devices. A problem has been recognized.

Possible Solution:

- Ensure that the colors are displayed accurately by adjusting the monitor's calibration. You have the option of utilizing operating system-integrated calibration tools or purchasing calibration software from a third party.
- It is advisable to verify the color profile parameters in Corel PaintShop Pro to ensure that they are adequately specified. Several parameters require meticulous consideration, including the grayscale, RGB, and CMYK profiles.
- When making modifications to photographs, ensure that color-managed procedures are utilized to maintain uniformity across multiple devices and products.
- It is imperative to verify that the printer is operating with the proper color profile and parameters corresponding to the desired output when handling print media.

- Should the issue of color accuracy persist, it would be prudent to consider implementing professional color management solutions or consulting with a color management expert.

CHAPTER TEN

WORKING WITH EFFECTS

CHOOSING EFFECTS

The Instant Effects palette, the Effect Browser, and the Effects submenu can be utilized to select effects. Individualize the majority of effects by modifying their parameters in the corresponding dialog boxes.

The dialog boxes utilized to apply effects share certain characteristics, including the following:

- In the Before pane, the initial image is presented; in the After pane, a sample of the image with the modified settings is showcased.

- The most recently utilized preset will be pre-selected in the Load Preset drop list. One can effortlessly apply consistent parameters to a variety of images by utilizing presets.

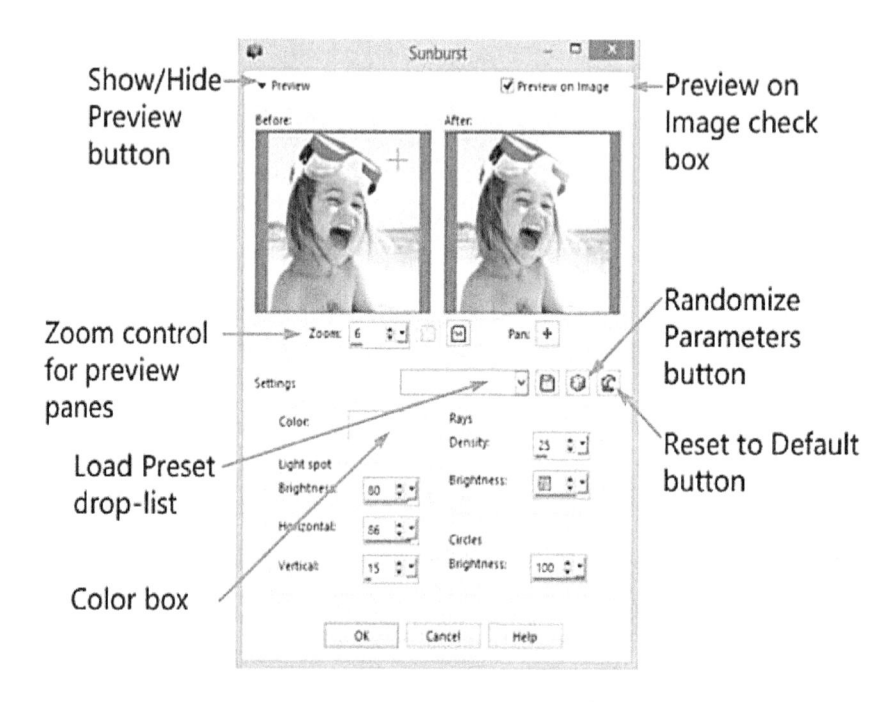

154

USE THE INSTANT EFFECTS PALETTE

By utilizing the Instant Effects palette, one can efficiently implement pre-established effects. If you prefer a straightforward approach, you can generate an effect using this straightforward method. Once the preset is complete, it will appear in the Instant Effects interface under the User Defined section after it was created in an effects dialog box. Customize the effect by modifying the Strength, Color Match, and Smooth Image parameters in the AI Style Transfer category.

USE THE EFFECT BROWSER

The Effect Browser can be of assistance when you wish to examine the effects that have been applied to your image before proceeding. In addition to presets generated by users and included with PaintShop Pro, the Effect Browser exhibits any additional presets that can be accessible.

In the Process Browser, PaintShop Pro employs both the effect's default preset and any additional presets that have been committed to the image when generating thumbnail previews. The preset is stored in a script-compatible file format (PspScript) for use with PaintShop Pro.

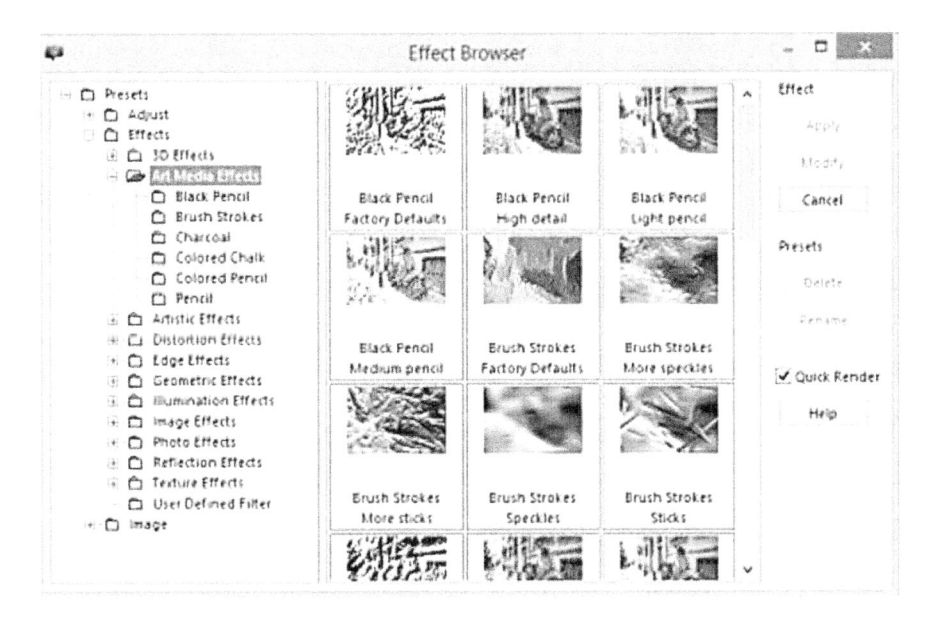

EMPLOY 3D EFFECTS

It is possible to generate designs or images that appear to have depth by utilizing 3D effects. When applied to the images utilized on web pages, these effects are extraordinarily useful.

USE BUTTONIZE

By applying the button-down effect to a selection, layer, or flattened image, it is possible to generate the visual impression of square or rectangular buttons. A three-dimensional border that generates the illusion of elevation will enhance your image. To access the Buttonize dialog box, select Buttonize from the **Effects > 3D Effects** drop-down menu in the top menu bar.

The Buttonize dialog box encompasses controls that govern a variety of settings.
- **Height:** The height value, denoted in pixels, serves to specify the button's height.
- **Width:** The value denoted in pixels and known as "Width" determines the breadth of the icon.
- **Opacity:** One way in which opacity contributes to the rounded appearance of a button is by introducing gentle shading along the button's edges.
- **Transparent:** The application of a solid color to the button's edges generates precise and distinct boundaries, thereby achieving transparency.
- **Solid:** This function applies a solid color to the button's edges to generate rounded edges. Utilize the Buttonize option from the drop-down menu after selecting a solid color to generate a button featuring a colored edge.
- **Color:** Select a hue to impart a particular aesthetic to the border of the icon. To choose a color, either right-click the color box or select it from the Recent Colors dialog box, respectively, in the Color dialog box. Both of these options are available to you.

USE CHISEL

The implementation of the Chisel effect creates the visual effect of a stone carving on a selection or layer through the use of a border that appears to be three-dimensional. You have the option of keeping the chiseled area the same color as the background or making it translucent to disclose the hues beneath. Simply select **Effects > 3D Effects > Chisel** from the Effects menu's drop-down menu to access the Chisel dialog box.

The Chisel dialog box encompasses controls for several settings.

- **Size:** By modifying this option, one can ascertain the overall pixel size of the incised region.
- **Transparent:** The incised area allows visibility of the underlying hues.
- **Solid color:** The entire area is rendered in a uniform shade of color.
- **Color:** An alternative color can be chosen to serve as the incised area's background. By selecting the desired color, the Color dialog box will be displayed for your use. You will be able to access the Recent Colors dialog box by right-clicking the color box.

MASTERING THE DROP SHADOW

Applying the Drop Shadow effect to the background of the current selection adds a shadow. One of the principal objectives is to impart a three-dimensional visual effect to text.

Before applying a drop shadow to an entire image, ensure that an adequate amount of negative space surrounds it. To complete this operation, navigate to the Image menu and select the Canvas Size or Add Borders option. To access the Drop Shadow dialog box, select 3D Effects from the Effects menu, followed by Drop Shadow.

The Drop Shadow dialog box contains controls for distinct settings.

- Position in the vertical plane dictates the magnitude of the shadow. By dragging the crosshair at the terminus of the offset indication line on the left side of the dialog box, the height can be modified.

- The shadow's breadth is determined by the horizontal line. By dragging the crosshair located at the terminus of the offset indication line on the dialog box's left, the width can be modified.
- The degree of shadow opacity is determined by opacity. By decreasing this value, the drop shadow will become less conspicuous.
- The degree of blurriness in the shadow is determined by the blur factor.
- The color of the drop shadow can be modified via the settings menu. To choose a color, either right-click the color box or select it from the Recent Colors dialog box, respectively, in the Color dialog box. Both of these options are available to you.
- Enable the drop shadow on an additional raster layer through the creation of a shadow on a novel layer.

To replicate the Drop Shadow effect, select the Border with drop shadow script from the Script toolbar's drop-list. An effect resembling the Drop Shadow effect will ensue.

Using the Inner Bevel

Apply the "Inner Bevel" three-dimensional effect to a selection or item surrounded by transparency to improve its appearance while preserving the object's original dimensions. The Inner Bevel effect's settings can be modified manually, from the preset effects included with the application, or by adjusting the parameters of a preset effect.

In the presence of a transparent backdrop, a colored background accompanied by a selection, or a colored background and a layer, the Inner Bevel function becomes operational on the corresponding image. In the absence of a transparent region or selection, the effect is implemented on the borders of the layer. Transparent layers can be generated through the utilization of the Eraser Tool, by pasting a selection as a new layer, or by promoting a selection. One should contemplate elevating a particular option to a higher level. Select **Inner Bevel** from the menu labeled **Effects > 3D Effects** to access the dialog box for this effect.

Here are the controls available in the dialog pane named "Inner Bevel:"
- **Bevel** describes the shape of the bevel.
- The **width** is denoted in pixels and requires a populated value.
- **Smoothness** regulates the thickness of the edge and the angle of the slope (sharpness). As the value within the range increases, the corners will progressively lose their sharpness. With each descent, the edges will become progressively more angular and pointed.
- The **depth** of the edge is determined and controlled by its profundity. By augmenting the value of this parameter, the edge will become more conspicuous.
- The **ambiance** is responsible for dynamically modifying the luminance of the image in transit.
- The reflectivity of a surface is influenced by its degree of sheen. Elevating the value will result in a heightened prominence of the highlights and an improved sheen to the image. As the value decreases, the visibility of the highlights diminishes.
- **Hue:** The color of the light that illuminates the image is determined by this attribute. You can access the Recent Colors dialog box by right-clicking the color box, selecting a color from the image, or opening the Color dialog box by clicking the color box. By carrying out any of these operations, the light will undergo a color modification.
- **Angle:** Angles facilitate the differentiation between illuminated and obscured edges. The direction of the light source can be deduced from the needle's position, which is quantified in degrees of rotation around the circle. To modify the value, one can select one of the following methods: manually enter a number into the control, click the circle, drag the needle, or type in the number.
- **Intensity:** The luminosity of the light emanating from a specific direction can be modified by utilizing the intensity function. Bear in mind that the Ambience parameter establishes the overall luminosity of the image before the application of the Intensity parameter.
- The **elevation** feature provides information regarding the angle at which the light source is situated within the image. At a 90-degree

angle, the light source is explicitly positioned above the object. The light source approaches the image as the value is decreased, resulting in the formation of elongated shadows.

Using Outer Bevel

The visual appeal of a selection by simulating raised edges, thereby producing a three-dimensional appearance. By executing this operation, the selection area is augmented by the length of the chamfer.

Before selecting the Outer Bevel option from the Effects menu, an area of the image must be selected. The Outer Bevel effect dialog box can be accessed by selecting 3D Effects from the Effects menu, followed by Outer Bevel from the drop-down menu.

Included in the Outer Bevel dialog box are the following options:
- **Bevel:** Descriptive of the bevel's shape.
- **Width:** Denoted in pixels, the width specifies the extent of the beveled edge.
- **Smoothness:** The degree of smoothness dictates both the severity or angle, of the slope and the thickness of the edge. A progressive deterioration in the precision of the corners will occur as the value increases within the range. As the object descends, the outlines become more pronounced and narrow.
- **Depth:** The height of the edge is determined by the depth. By augmenting the value of this parameter, the edge will become more conspicuous.
- **Ambiance:** The luminosity of the image is modified following the ambient.
- **Color:** This attribute establishes the tone of the light that casts illumination on the image. You can access the Recent Colors dialog box by right-clicking the color box, selecting a color from the image, or opening the Color dialog box by clicking the color box. By carrying out any of these operations, the light will undergo a color modification.

- **Angle:** Angle plays a critical role in determining which edges are illuminated and which are obscured. The direction of the light source is indicated by the needle's position, which is quantified in degrees of rotation around the circle. The value can be modified in many ways, including by selecting the circle, dragging the needle, manually entering a number into the control, or typing in a number.
- **Intensity:** The luminosity of the light emanating from the specified direction can be modified by adjusting the intensity setting. Bear in mind that the Ambience parameter establishes the overall luminosity of the image before the addition of the Intensity parameter.
- **Elevation:** The angle at which the light source is situated in relation to the image is denoted by the elevation. At a 90-degree angle, the light source is explicitly positioned above the object. The light source approaches the image as the value is decreased, resulting in the formation of elongated shadows.

Using Brush Strokes

The Brush Strokes effect imparts the visual impression that your image is rendered in oil or watercolor. In the Effects drop-down menu, navigate to Brush Strokes > Art Media Effects > Brush Strokes to access the Brush Strokes dialog box.

Within the Brush Stroke dialog box, the following options are editable:
- The level of blurring implemented on an image is determined by its softness.
- The bristle number is indicated on the brush.
- Adjust the width of the brush proportionately.
- Opacity regulates the magnitude of the effect.
- The size of the brushstrokes is denoted by the length.
- The number of strokes employed in the image dictates the density of the strokes.
- To ascertain which edges are illuminated and which are not, one must contemplate the angle. The direction of the light source is indicated by the needle's position, which is quantified in degrees of rotation around

the circle. The value can be modified in several ways, including by selecting the circle, dragging the needle, manually entering a number into the control, or typing in a number.

- A color can be chosen to reflect light along the formations' contours. By selecting the desired color, the Color dialog box will be displayed for your use. Right-clicking the color box will reveal the Recent Colors dialog box, which can be utilized.

Using Charcoal

The Charcoal effect is comparable to the Black Pencil effect; however, the resultant image exhibits reduced detail as a consequence of the denser brushstrokes. Navigate to **Effects > Art Media Effects > Charcoal** via the drop-down menu to access the Charcoal dialog box.

The dialog pane of the Charcoal effect comprises the following controls:

- **Detail:** Each stroke's intensity and quantity are determined by the level of detail.

- **Opacity:** The control that dictates the strength of the impact is opacity. By augmenting the opacity value, the effect in the image is intensified at the expense of its initial visual appeal.

Using Colored Pencil

The Colored Pencil effect generates the illusion that the subject was rendered with colored pencils by utilizing the hues that are already present in the image. With finer strokes, this effect closely resembles the Colored Chalk effect.

To access the Colored Pencil dialog box, click Effects, then Art Media Effects, and ultimately Colored Pencil from the drop-down menu.

The numerous option controls are displayed in the Colored Pencil dialog box.

- **Detail**: is tasked with the computation of both the quantity and intensity of strokes.

- **Opacity controls** the strength of the effect. By increasing the opacity value, the effect in the image is intensified at the expense of its original appearance.

Using Pencil

The Pencil effect is a visual enhancement that combines color addition and edge sharpening to convert an image into the appearance of a realistic pencil sketch. To access the Pencil dialog box, utilize the Effects menu's drop-down menu and select **Effects > Art Media Effects > Pencil**.

The following options are represented by controls in the Pencil dialog box:

- **Luminance:** The function of luminance is to modify the luminosity of the image.

- **Blur:** Blur quantifies the degree to which an image appears out of focus. A decline in the image's resolution is observed as the value increases.

- **Color:** When choosing a color for the background of an image, one is provided with the option to select the area that does not have any edges as a border. You can right-click the color box to access the Recent Colors dialog box, select a color from the image, or select the color box to access the Color dialog box. Participating in any of these activities will induce a modification in the hue of the light.

- **Intensity:** The contrast between the image's boundaries and the background is determined by the intensity level. By increasing the contrast, further details become apparent.

CONCLUSION

Within the world of photo editing software, Corel PaintShop Pro emerges as a preeminent and groundbreaking application. This remarkable editing program allows you to modify your images with ease and is available for a very reasonable price. It is a dependable application that offers advanced editing functionalities through the implementation of an extensive range of tools. By utilizing the Refine Brush Tool, one can effortlessly execute a complex selection. A significant amount of prior experience with editing is not required to operate this program. Additionally, it is the most economical alternative. Utilize the most recent Corel software to generate an aesthetically pleasing image at a remarkably low cost.

INDEX

aberration, 100, 101, 103

accommodate, 50, 72

account, 16, 17

additional, 22, 27, 29, 43, 49, 67, 102, 114, 126, 129, 137, 143, 164, 168, 172, 177, 180

Additionally, 14, 16, 17, 21, 22, 24, 29, 34, 36, 39, 45, 53, 71, 72, 93, 131, 133, 140, 143, 145, 150, 164, 186

adjacent, 47, 75, 93, 125, 126, 133, 135, 137, 138, 142, 151, 156

adjustment, 31, 71, 81, 93, 95, 104, 109, 114, 115, 116, 118, 121, 123, 124, 164

Adjustment, 31, 42, 43, 111, 117, 164

adjustments, 21, 26, 32, 53, 66, 67, 74, 80, 81, 90, 92, 99, 107, 108, 109, 110, 118, 123, 131, 139, 155, 164, 168

administrative, 17, 170

administrator, 17, 170

advanced, 13, 80, 86, 92, 167, 186

aesthetic, 42, 137, 153, 167, 178

AfterShot, 14

AI power, 13

Airbrushes, 42

alterations, 21, 67, 91, 164

apertures, 25, 47

appearance, 21, 42, 43, 55, 100, 102, 105, 109, 112, 114, 117, 127, 135, 136, 137, 154, 155, 167, 178, 180, 182, 185

application, 16, 18, 30, 32, 34, 59, 60, 70, 80, 81, 83, 89, 96, 103, 120, 134, 139, 145, 152, 156, 157, 161, 163, 167, 168, 171, 172, 178, 180, 182, 186

applications, 16, 17, 39, 40, 60, 68, 70, 71, 96, 125, 152, 156, 164, 168, 169

Automated, 41

automatically, 16, 18, 20, 41, 44, 46, 48, 59, 80, 83, 86, 90, 103, 115

available, 15, 16, 17, 22, 26, 27, 36, 47, 49, 54, 57, 63, 66, 70, 78, 102, 103, 107, 120, 127, 131, 153, 154, 155, 162, 164, 166, 169, 170, 171, 178, 180, 181, 186

Aware, 15

azure, 125

background, 23, 24, 35, 41, 42, 43, 76, 93, 95, 118, 135, 145, 146, 151, 154, 155, 160, 179, 180, 186

Background, 4, 14, 23, 35, 148, 152, 154, 155

Backspace, 49

beneath, 21, 48, 73, 124, 150, 151, 179
Blemish, 42
Blend, 37, 136
blending, 109, 147, 164, 165
blocky, 126
blooming, 100, 101
blurriness, 100, 128, 132, 156, 180
borders, 102, 134, 153, 167, 180
boxes, 26, 46, 47, 77, 78, 91, 124, 143, 175
brightness, 22, 42, 66, 91, 92, 114, 118, 133, 141, 164
brush, 24, 36, 41, 82, 146, 153, 165, 170, 171, 184
Brush, 12, 14, 36, 37, 40, 41, 42, 163, 165, 170, 183, 184, 186
brushstrokes, 55, 74, 184
Burn, 42, 43
cacophony, 125
calendars, 153
camera, 27, 36, 59, 60, 64, 79, 81, 88, 97, 100, 102, 103, 105, 106, 118, 134, 137, 142
Camera, 5, 63, 64, 65, 66, 67, 104, 125
cameras, 63, 67, 70, 81, 96, 100, 111, 134
Cancel, 33, 66, 89
capabilities, 13, 14, 15, 24, 26, 28, 80, 139, 165, 167, 168
capability, 36, 47, 64, 66, 67, 164
capture, 63, 80, 100, 103, 111, 125, 131, 134

Capture, 14
Capturing, 79
cards, 153
catalog, 83, 84, 86
categories, 27, 84
category, 19, 32, 34, 161, 176
CD, 153
Center, 37, 38
Channel, 108, 114
checkbox, 20, 33, 37, 39, 48, 62, 66, 78, 82, 92, 93, 99, 108, 115, 124, 128, 130, 141, 142, 143, 145, 155, 156
chromatic, 100, 103
Chromatic, 100
clicking, 19, 31, 39, 41, 43, 46, 49, 54, 58, 68, 71, 81, 84, 86, 101, 112, 114, 151, 155, 158, 160, 161, 162, 179, 181, 183, 184
clipping, 20, 115
Clone, 40, 42
Cloning, 15
collection, 16, 27, 31, 67, 87, 155, 166
Collections, 27, 59, 83, 84, 85, 86, 87
color, 13, 14, 16, 20, 29, 34, 35, 41, 43, 49, 55, 57, 59, 60, 62, 66, 80, 90, 93, 94, 95, 96, 97, 99, 101, 103, 107, 108, 109, 114, 115, 116, 117, 118, 119, 120, 121, 122, 123, 124, 125, 126, 127, 128, 133, 134, 135, 138, 144, 145, 146, 147, 149, 150, 151,

153, 157, 158, 159, 165, 166, 174, 178, 179, 180, 181, 183, 184, 185, 186
Color, 4, 5, 8, 10, 11, 12, 34, 35, 43, 47, 49, 57, 58, 59, 108, 109, 114, 115, 121, 146, 147, 150, 156, 157, 158, 174, 176, 178, 179, 180, 181, 183, 184, 186
colors, 37, 42, 43, 47, 56, 74, 92, 93, 100, 103, 107, 115, 121, 122, 123, 124, 125, 138, 144, 149, 151, 157, 174
command, 35, 38, 46, 47, 53, 54, 60, 70, 75, 76, 77, 78, 79, 89, 90, 96, 97, 119, 121, 126, 129, 136, 137, 138, 139
commands, 29, 31, 39, 46, 53, 70, 75, 76, 127, 129, 133, 134, 135
comparison, 15, 63, 126, 142
compatibility, 16, 17, 169, 172
Complete, 16, 20, 26, 27, 32, 33, 84
completion, 37
composite, 14, 20, 114
compositions, 13
comprehensive, 15, 26, 27, 37, 53, 138, 168
computation, 126, 185
conduct, 33, 49, 86, 165, 168
configuration, 26, 33, 47, 66, 71, 75, 78, 92, 110, 112, 124, 131, 142, 161, 170, 171
configurations, 37, 46, 47, 57, 64, 67, 79, 81, 89, 91, 92, 110, 125, 156, 166

Configure, 89
contains, 16, 29, 31, 40, 90, 103, 179
Content, 15
contribute, 100
control, 49, 57, 58, 72, 74, 78, 79, 92, 93, 94, 95, 101, 105, 106, 108, 109, 112, 113, 114, 116, 117, 120, 121, 123, 124, 127, 128, 130, 131, 136, 137, 141, 156, 168, 182, 183, 184, 185
controllers, 35
controls, 20, 21, 26, 31, 47, 75, 80, 81, 89, 90, 92, 99, 102, 103, 108, 115, 116, 122, 141, 154, 155, 178, 179, 181, 184, 185
Corel, 1, 13, 14, 15, 16, 17, 19, 22, 23, 64, 67, 102, 131, 133, 135, 142, 144, 157, 158, 161, 162, 163, 165, 166, 167, 168, 169, 170, 171, 172, 173, 174, 186
correction, 16, 20, 79, 89, 90, 99, 101, 102, 103, 104, 116, 131, 135
Correction, 13, 42, 88, 89, 102, 103, 105, 106, 109, 131
corresponding, 19, 49, 51, 77, 93, 108, 115, 116, 124, 132, 159, 174, 175, 180
covers, 137, 153
creation, 13, 39, 60, 64, 124, 157, 161, 164, 166, 180
Crop, 22, 40, 42, 89
cursor, 29, 45, 46, 48, 53, 73, 82, 83, 115, 146, 159

customizable, 22, 36, 55, 149
Customization, 82
customized, 40, 157, 162
deactivate, 35, 73, 143
decrease, 60, 61, 92, 94, 124, 132, 154, 156, 169
Delete, 49, 93, 126, 149, 169
denotes, 103, 110, 126, 144, 156
design, 13, 15, 34, 56, 60, 144, 147, 153, 156, 157
Despeckle, 129
details, 2, 26, 27, 36, 38, 60, 71, 86, 126, 128, 129, 135, 136, 137, 143, 186
Determine, 101, 127, 129, 130
Determining, 55, 143
digital, 2, 13, 15, 20, 42, 60, 63, 66, 70, 79, 95, 96, 97, 100, 111, 120, 126, 134, 161
dimensions, 29, 34, 38, 45, 53, 61, 71, 90, 106, 132, 137, 138, 139, 140, 141, 142, 143, 161, 169, 180
directives, 28, 29, 74
discovery, 27
distinct, 15, 42, 46, 67, 100, 124, 125, 126, 128, 135, 144, 162, 165, 178, 179
distinguishes, 120, 126
distinguishing, 31
distorted, 42, 105
distortion, 13, 88, 102, 103, 104, 105, 120, 142
disturbance, 125, 129
docked, 35, 38

Dodge, 42
dragging, 38, 40, 42, 43, 44, 45, 53, 74, 90, 101, 109, 115, 124, 132, 139, 180, 183, 184
Dropper, 41, 115, 145, 146
DVD, 18
Edge, 129, 164, 165
Edit, 3, 4, 24, 28, 32, 38, 39, 40, 44, 45, 48, 49, 50, 55, 64, 65, 67, 70, 76, 79, 80, 91, 117, 118, 122, 131
edition, 14
editor, 13, 68, 151
effects, 13, 22, 29, 31, 37, 38, 42, 47, 61, 74, 102, 118, 120, 147, 166, 167, 175, 176, 177, 180
Effects, 21, 24, 29, 31, 34, 37, 38, 81, 175, 176, 178, 179, 181, 182, 183, 184, 185
efficiency, 27, 161, 162
Elevating, 156, 181
eliminate, 42, 126, 133, 150
elimination, 128, 129
enhancing, 13, 14, 30, 39, 42, 167, 168
enlarged, 82, 102, 118, 138, 141
eradicate, 128
Essentials, 14, 16, 20, 26
execution, 36, 37, 39, 74, 75
EXIF, 28, 37, 60, 86
facilitate, 15, 16, 29, 31, 37, 46, 68, 157, 166, 181
features, 14, 15, 17, 26, 33, 47, 80, 95, 162, 169
Files, 6, 29, 68, 69

Fill, 43, 94, 95, 112, 113, 145, 146, 148, 152, 154, 155
film, 22, 100, 126, 134, 167
Fix, 21, 46, 90, 91, 92, 111
Focus, 14, 46, 92, 132
folder, 27, 59, 62, 68, 83, 84, 85, 86, 152, 153, 157, 159, 162
foreground, 41, 43, 145, 146, 151, 153, 155, 160
Frame, 14, 15, 20, 44
Freehand, 41, 132, 163
fresh, 27, 85, 150, 159, 164, 170
function, 16, 21, 34, 40, 41, 43, 61, 71, 75, 76, 78, 81, 91, 100, 101, 114, 126, 128, 130, 134, 138, 164, 178, 180, 182, 185
functions, 16, 17, 40, 64, 111, 128
gallery, 80
General, 55, 62, 78, 141
generate, 20, 28, 37, 101, 107, 118, 121, 147, 149, 155, 163, 164, 176, 177, 178, 186
Gradient, 43, 148, 149, 150, 151, 152, 153, 156
Gradually, 128
granted, 157, 164
graph, 99, 111, 114, 115, 117, 118
graphic, 13, 161, 166
graphical, 36
graphics, 153, 169, 171
green, 36, 96, 99, 107, 109, 114, 121, 123, 125, 144
grids, 55

group, 44, 57, 62, 92, 99, 105, 106, 108, 115, 117, 124
guide, 20, 22, 55, 57, 58, 59, 168
guidelines, 55, 86, 107, 110
guides, 55
Guides, 5, 55, 58, 59
hardware, 34
histogram, 20, 110, 111, 114, 115, 116, 117, 118
horizontal, 53, 55, 57, 58, 90, 111, 118, 180
hues, 20, 56, 93, 96, 106, 107, 120, 121, 135, 138, 145, 147, 149, 150, 151, 154, 157, 165, 179, 185
icon, 13, 16, 20, 27, 31, 32, 33, 38, 45, 46, 47, 49, 51, 52, 65, 66, 67, 68, 74, 75, 76, 77, 79, 81, 83, 87, 115, 116, 124, 142, 145, 146, 147, 148, 149, 151, 154, 155, 156, 158, 159, 160, 161, 165, 178
iconography, 33
illuminated, 66, 113, 118, 181, 183, 184
illustrate, 36, 99, 107, 166
image, 5, 13, 14, 15, 22, 23, 26, 27, 29, 31, 34, 35, 36, 37, 39, 40, 42, 43, 44, 47, 48, 49, 50, 51, 52, 53, 54, 55, 57, 59, 60, 61, 63, 64, 65, 66, 67, 68, 69, 70, 71, 72, 73, 74, 75, 77, 78, 79, 80, 81, 82, 83, 85, 87, 89, 90, 91, 93, 94, 95, 96, 97, 99, 100, 101, 102, 103, 104, 105, 106, 107, 108, 109, 110, 111, 112, 113, 114, 115, 116, 117,

118, 119, 120, 121, 122, 124, 125, 126, 128, 129, 130, 133, 134, 135, 136, 137, 138, 139, 141, 142, 143, 145, 146, 152, 153, 154, 155, 156, 157, 161, 163, 164, 165, 167, 168, 169, 172, 173, 176, 177, 178, 179, 180, 181, 182, 183, 184, 185, 186
Image, 4, 5, 6, 7, 9, 10, 24, 47, 48, 50, 51, 52, 53, 59, 73, 74, 86, 90, 95, 99, 107, 115, 121, 129, 134, 139, 142, 145, 154, 176, 179
images, 15, 16, 20, 26, 28, 29, 30, 31, 36, 39, 40, 42, 43, 44, 46, 49, 55, 59, 60, 61, 62, 64, 66, 67, 70, 71, 78, 79, 80, 83, 84, 85, 86, 92, 93, 95, 96, 97, 100, 101, 102, 104, 107, 110, 118, 119, 133, 134, 135, 136, 137, 142, 143, 144, 161, 164, 166, 167, 168, 173, 176, 177, 186
increases, 95, 121, 156, 181, 182, 185
indicated, 73, 78, 83, 117, 132, 183, 184
indispensable, 30, 153, 163
information, 26, 27, 33, 37, 39, 60, 68, 69, 81, 83, 84, 85, 103, 113, 118, 126, 138, 182
installation, 16, 17, 19, 170
Instant, 21, 22, 31, 34, 37, 81, 175, 176
instructions, 19, 20, 35, 38, 70, 74, 75, 79, 127

instrument, 33, 39, 80, 156
instruments, 15, 26, 28, 31, 33, 39, 40, 165, 170
integration, 42
integrity, 126, 129, 150
interface, 13, 16, 24, 36, 39, 45, 53, 62, 68, 80, 81, 83, 90, 145, 155, 159, 160, 171, 176
interfaces, 82
interruptions, 17, 162
JPEG, 60, 62, 63, 64, 67, 104, 125, 126, 142
known, 20, 21, 46, 165, 178
Layer, 7, 90, 164, 165
luminance, 36, 42, 94, 108, 110, 114, 117, 120, 121, 124, 126, 133, 137, 181, 185
luminosity, 13, 43, 92, 107, 110, 117, 118, 124, 182, 183, 185
Magic, 41, 163
magnification, 37, 50, 71, 72, 73, 99, 100, 102, 112, 114
magnifier, 73
Magnifier, 73
magnitude, 42, 101, 104, 154, 156, 180, 184
malfunctions, 96, 125
manipulating, 36, 45, 82, 121, 134
Manually, 18, 110, 124
Material, 152, 154, 155, 157
Max, 118
Menu, 5, 29, 54
midtones, 36, 118
miniature, 34, 40

minimal, 17, 26
minimum, 55, 100, 109, 113, 118, 128, 129, 130, 137, 169
Mixer, 37, 108
mode, 14, 24, 49, 60, 63, 67, 73, 80, 82, 104, 111, 136, 145, 167
modification, 15, 16, 22, 26, 29, 33, 37, 39, 42, 47, 60, 88, 114, 151, 161, 171, 181, 183, 186
modifications, 30, 33, 47, 50, 52, 57, 64, 66, 67, 68, 74, 78, 80, 81, 91, 105, 106, 108, 114, 116, 121, 125, 150, 164, 168, 174
Modifications, 6, 48, 81, 118
modify, 28, 35, 37, 38, 43, 44, 45, 46, 49, 52, 55, 62, 66, 67, 68, 74, 78, 80, 81, 82, 90, 91, 92, 94, 95, 99, 104, 105, 106, 110, 111, 112, 114, 115, 116, 117, 118, 121, 122, 123, 124, 128, 132, 133, 138, 140, 141, 142, 143, 146, 149, 150, 152, 154, 156, 161, 162, 163, 164, 168, 171, 181, 185, 186
Moire, 128, 129
Move, 4, 40, 41, 45, 146
MultiCam, 14
multitude, 28, 79, 87, 100, 161, 171
Navigate, 52, 54, 57, 61, 66, 68, 69, 71, 74, 81, 99, 121, 124, 129, 130, 131, 153, 154, 156, 184
navigating, 46, 57, 59, 89, 156, 157, 159

Navigation, 59, 82, 83, 84, 85, 86
neighbors, 126
Noise, 8, 9, 66, 96, 97, 99, 125, 127, 128, 129, 130, 131
numerals, 56
numerous, 16, 37, 84, 111, 123, 125, 154, 162, 185
Objects, 14
online, 60, 153
opacity, 83, 150, 151, 171, 178, 180, 185
operations, 20, 29, 31, 36, 74, 77, 78, 79, 82, 100, 107, 110, 162, 166, 181, 183
option, 16, 17, 21, 25, 26, 33, 39, 47, 52, 56, 59, 61, 62, 63, 65, 66, 68, 69, 71, 72, 73, 74, 75, 77, 78, 81, 82, 85, 87, 89, 90, 92, 93, 98, 102, 106, 107, 109, 115, 117, 122, 123, 124, 127, 128, 131, 136, 140, 141, 142, 143, 146, 150, 156, 157, 158, 160, 161, 164, 170, 171, 174, 178, 179, 181, 182, 185, 186
organizer, 28, 37
Organizer, 27, 31, 37, 53, 54, 59, 65, 68, 80, 81, 82, 83, 84, 85
organizing, 27, 35, 84
outcomes, 21, 37, 75, 121, 129, 166
Painter, 14
painting, 36, 37, 39, 42, 153
Paintshop, 15, 16

PaintShop, 1, 13, 14, 15, 16, 17, 19, 20, 21, 22, 23, 26, 32, 35, 46, 53, 59, 60, 61, 64, 67, 71, 80, 86, 95, 96, 102, 104, 107, 110, 111, 120, 125, 127, 131, 133, 135, 137, 142, 144, 145, 152, 153, 155, 156, 157, 158, 159, 161, 162, 163, 165, 166, 167, 168, 169, 170, 171, 172, 173, 174, 177, 186

palette, 20, 27, 31, 34, 35, 36, 37, 38, 44, 45, 46, 50, 53, 54, 56, 57, 59, 65, 74, 75, 76, 77, 80, 82, 83, 84, 85, 86, 89, 148, 151, 155, 157, 158, 159, 160, 175, 176

Palettes, 7, 11, 20, 29, 35, 37, 44, 83, 111, 158

Pan, 4, 6, 40, 47, 48, 53, 73, 74, 101

pane, 32, 38, 39, 40, 48, 49, 51, 55, 59, 64, 65, 66, 67, 69, 80, 82, 83, 84, 87, 91, 93, 99, 100, 101, 109, 115, 122, 128, 146, 152, 159, 176, 181, 184

panel, 21, 59, 72, 74, 78, 81, 83, 86, 89, 90, 115, 145, 146, 152, 153, 156, 158, 159, 160, 165

panes, 47, 50, 100, 112, 114, 116, 117

parameter, 47, 103, 104, 105, 129, 141, 181, 182, 183

parameters, 33, 36, 37, 47, 49, 62, 67, 68, 90, 92, 97, 99, 103, 104, 109, 113, 122, 124, 141, 146, 152, 156, 164, 171, 173, 174, 175, 176, 180

particles, 126, 129, 130, 151

Pattern, 10, 128, 129, 154, 156

patterns, 14, 126, 128, 131, 153, 155, 157

Patterns, 9, 128, 153

pavement, 155

Pen, 40, 44

percentages, 13

performance, 14, 17, 34, 169

permissions, 17

Perspective, 7, 42, 88, 89, 90

photo, 13, 15, 16, 22, 23, 27, 31, 36, 66, 68, 69, 80, 90, 92, 93, 134, 186

Photo, 21, 24, 46, 90, 91, 92, 111

photograph, 20, 21, 22, 24, 27, 31, 95, 97, 100, 105, 107, 110, 116, 137

photographs, 13, 15, 16, 21, 37, 38, 39, 42, 50, 60, 61, 67, 80, 86, 87, 90, 93, 95, 97, 102, 120, 125, 126, 136, 137, 164, 166, 167, 174

photography, 26, 33, 34, 60, 93, 96

Photography, 16, 20, 24, 26, 32, 33

photos, 27, 32, 39, 67, 71, 84

pigments, 37

pixels, 13, 41, 43, 55, 58, 93, 101, 105, 110, 111, 117, 118, 119, 121, 125, 126, 127, 128, 130, 133, 134, 135, 136, 137, 138, 140, 141, 142, 143, 145, 178, 181, 182

PlayStation, 16

Portable, 16

possibility, 154
practical, 13, 38, 162
preconfigured, 26
predetermined, 41, 55
preferences, 14, 26, 66, 82, 83, 162, 163, 170, 171
Preferences, 55, 62, 78, 141, 159, 163
present, 26, 34, 36, 40, 42, 47, 68, 84, 93, 101, 108, 111, 117, 126, 137, 141, 143, 169, 185
presentation, 70, 156
Presenting, 37, 41, 156
presets, 13, 116, 166, 176, 177
preview, 22, 27, 34, 47, 66, 74, 82, 155, 156
Preview, 4, 7, 31, 47, 48, 53, 66, 82, 87, 115
Previews, 47
print, 13, 37, 142, 173, 174
Pro, 1, 13, 14, 15, 16, 17, 19, 20, 26, 32, 35, 46, 53, 59, 60, 61, 64, 67, 71, 80, 86, 95, 96, 102, 104, 107, 110, 111, 120, 125, 127, 131, 133, 135, 137, 142, 144, 145, 152, 153, 155, 156, 157, 158, 161, 162, 163, 165, 166, 167, 168, 169, 170, 171, 172, 173, 174, 177, 186
problematic, 129, 130
procedure, 17, 19, 23, 59, 69, 79, 84, 97, 128
productivity, 13, 70, 71, 162
products, 153, 174

professionals, 13, 60
program, 14, 15, 16, 19, 20, 23, 59, 60, 71, 74, 99, 126, 144, 167, 168, 172, 173, 186
Program, 55, 62, 78, 141
programs, 17, 145
Programs, 19
project, 27
projects, 13, 153, 157
promotional, 26
Properties, 5, 56, 90, 148, 152, 153, 154, 155, 157
prototype, 14
punctuation, 56
RAW, 5, 6, 60, 63, 64, 65, 66, 67, 68, 69, 104
recently, 27, 62, 74, 75, 80, 148, 155, 176
rectification, 42
Red, 42, 46, 103, 108, 109, 114
Refined, 15
reflected, 48, 72, 99
regions, 13, 42, 66, 81, 82, 93, 94, 95, 97, 101, 109, 110, 113, 115, 120, 126, 131, 134, 147, 163, 164, 165
reinstate, 128
remember, 38, 53, 71, 142
Removal, 8, 42, 46, 96, 97, 99, 100, 127, 128, 129
remove, 84, 87, 89, 93, 102, 107, 115, 126, 141, 149
Remove, 7, 9, 10, 82, 85, 87, 99, 115, 127, 128, 129, 130, 131, 149

Remover, 13, 42
renders, 13, 93
repairing, 13, 134
Replacement, 14, 23
replete, 26
representation, 36, 50, 120, 124, 154, 174
reshaping, 41
resize, 50, 53, 139, 141, 162
resizing, 13, 38, 44, 71, 83, 139, 140, 141
resolves, 42, 171
restoring, 13
retouching, 37, 167
reverse, 36, 74, 75, 76, 77, 82
rotation, 22, 41, 124, 181, 183, 184
routine, 38
rulers, 55, 57
runs, 17
Scratch, 13, 42
script, 36, 37, 39, 79, 177, 180
scroll, 53, 72
segmented, 27, 36
selecting, 16, 20, 24, 27, 32, 33, 35, 39, 40, 41, 43, 46, 47, 49, 51, 52, 53, 54, 57, 59, 62, 65, 66, 68, 71, 72, 74, 75, 77, 78, 79, 80, 81, 82, 84, 85, 90, 91, 96, 99, 103, 106, 108, 111, 117, 118, 122, 124, 125, 127, 128, 130, 136, 142, 144, 146, 150, 151, 152,153, 156, 157, 159, 160, 161, 170, 178, 179, 181, 182, 183, 184

selection, 13, 24, 29, 30, 40, 41, 43, 47, 48, 49, 56, 82, 92, 103, 110, 114, 120, 124, 130, 131, 132, 133, 134, 135, 139, 146, 151, 163, 164, 165, 166, 178, 179, 180, 182, 186
Selection, 10, 15, 41, 81, 82, 132, 154, 163, 165, 166
selections, 47, 55, 163
Selective, 46
Sensor, 100
settings, 27, 34, 36, 42, 46, 47, 49, 57, 62, 66, 67, 68, 92, 97, 103, 108, 116, 118, 136, 137, 145, 166, 170, 171, 176, 178, 179, 180
Setup, 18
shape, 20, 41, 44, 89, 131, 163, 181, 182
sharing, 16, 60, 135
Show, 4, 37, 47, 59, 76
sketching, 37
slider, 21, 49, 66, 82, 92, 93, 94, 95, 98, 107, 108, 117, 118, 123, 124, 129, 132, 143
Smart, 21, 41, 42, 46, 86, 87, 90, 91, 92, 107, 111, 165, 166
smooth, 134, 165
Smooth, 129, 131, 176
snap, 55, 57
Snap, 14, 57, 90
software, 13, 14, 15, 16, 17, 41, 42, 59, 60, 61, 70, 96, 103, 126, 152, 162, 168, 169, 170, 172, 173, 174, 186

Software, 16
solutions, 13, 142, 174
space, 47, 61, 78, 117, 150, 179
Spacebar, 53, 74
Special, 70, 138, 139
spectrum, 34, 101, 110, 119, 126
speed, 13, 78, 134
Stacking, 14
Standard, 33, 39, 62, 76, 79
status, 29, 38, 39
storage, 62, 78, 157
Straighten, 42
stratum, 138, 164
streamlined, 17, 33
Strength, 94, 95, 98, 104, 105, 106, 113, 176
stroke, 41, 43, 184
Stroke, 148, 153, 155, 184
supplementary, 2, 38, 91
symmetric, 20
tasks, 26, 39, 40, 144, 162
taxing, 79
telephoto, 100
temperature, 107, 108
temporarily, 34
Text, 20, 40, 44
texture, 42, 125, 126, 127, 144, 154, 155, 156, 157, 165
texture's, 155, 156
thumbnail, 34, 37, 50, 54, 65, 67, 68, 69, 80, 82, 154, 157, 177
thumbnails, 27, 31, 37, 65, 68, 69, 84, 157, 161

tool, 13, 15, 16, 20, 22, 23, 29, 35, 36, 37, 40, 41, 42, 53, 66, 72, 73, 74, 81, 88, 89, 90, 146, 152, 156, 163, 164, 166, 171
Tool, 10, 12, 14, 15, 20, 37, 44, 72, 74, 89, 145, 163, 166, 170, 180, 186
toolbar, 20, 28, 31, 33, 34, 39, 40, 42, 45, 46, 54, 72, 73, 76, 79, 81, 83, 152, 180
toolbars, 26, 29, 35, 38, 39, 44, 45, 56, 162
Toolbars, 29, 39
tools, 13, 15, 22, 23, 26, 27, 28, 30, 31, 33, 37, 39, 40, 42, 53, 60, 67, 80, 83, 84, 86, 96, 132, 146, 156, 162, 163, 164, 165, 166, 167, 168, 174, 186
tooltip, 38, 159
Toothbrush, 42
Traditional, 16
transform, 119, 121, 154
transformed, 20, 75
underexposed, 93, 111
undertones, 125
Uninstall, 19
uninstalling, 20
update, 14, 68, 115
upgraded, 15
users, 16, 17, 20, 26, 27, 33, 64, 72, 75, 86, 92, 111, 145, 153, 162, 163, 164, 166, 177
Variance, 36

variety, 22, 26, 29, 35, 40, 42, 71, 92, 125, 139, 144, 145, 153, 156, 162, 164, 166, 176, 178
various, 13, 24, 47, 49, 50, 60, 102, 125, 133, 138, 139, 153, 154, 166
vector, 20, 40, 41, 53, 152
versatile, 13, 161
vertical, 52, 53, 55, 58, 90, 111, 118, 180
vignette, 102, 103, 167
visibility, 28, 45, 46, 71, 83, 90, 125, 128, 145, 179, 181

Wand, 41, 163
Welcome, 3, 20, 26, 32
Windows, 5, 16, 17, 19, 46, 52, 59, 70, 145
workspace, 20, 24, 26, 27, 28, 32, 33, 34, 44, 71, 162, 171
Workspace, 12, 15, 16, 20, 34, 35, 162, 171
workspaces, 16, 20, 21, 26, 32, 34
zoom, 71, 100, 101, 116, 117, 128
Zoom, 6, 40, 47, 53, 72, 73, 74, 128

A

aberration, 100, 101, 103
accommodate, 50, 72
account, 16, 17
additional, 22, 27, 29, 43, 49, 67, 102, 114, 126, 129, 137, 143, 164, 168, 172, 177, 180
Additionally, 14, 16, 17, 21, 22, 24, 29, 34, 36, 39, 45, 53, 71, 72, 93, 131, 133, 140, 143, 145, 150, 164, 186
adjacent, 47, 75, 93, 125, 126, 133, 135, 137, 138, 142, 151, 156
adjustment, 31, 71, 81, 93, 95, 104, 109, 114, 115, 116, 118, 121, 123, 124, 164
Adjustment, 31, 42, 43, 111, 117, 164

adjustments, 21, 26, 32, 53, 66, 67, 74, 80, 81, 90, 92, 99, 107, 108, 109, 110, 118, 123, 131, 139, 155, 164, 168
administrative, 17, 170
administrator, 17, 170
advanced, 13, 80, 86, 92, 167, 186
aesthetic, 42, 137, 153, 167, 178
AfterShot, 14
AI power, 13
Airbrushes, 42
alterations, 21, 67, 91, 164
apertures, 25, 47
appearance, 21, 42, 43, 55, 100, 102, 105, 109, 112, 114, 117, 127, 135, 136, 137, 154, 155, 167, 178, 180, 182, 185
application, 16, 18, 30, 32, 34, 59, 60, 70, 80, 81, 83, 89, 96, 103, 120, 134, 139, 145, 152, 156,

157, 161, 163, 167, 168, 171, 172, 178, 180, 182, 186
applications, 16, 17, 39, 40, 60, 68, 70, 71, 96, 125, 152, 156, 164, 168, 169
Automated, 41
automatically, 16, 18, 20, 41, 44, 46, 48, 59, 80, 83, 86, 90, 103, 115
available, 15, 16, 17, 22, 26, 27, 36, 47, 49, 54, 57, 63, 66, 70, 78, 102, 103, 107, 120, 127, 131, 153, 154, 155, 162, 164, 166, 169, 170, 171, 178, 180, 181, 186
Aware, 15
azure, 125

B

background, 23, 24, 35, 41, 42, 43, 76, 93, 95, 118, 135, 145, 146, 151, 154, 155, 160, 179, 180, 186
Background, 4, 14, 23, 35, 148, 152, 154, 155
Backspace, 49
beneath, 21, 48, 73, 124, 150, 151, 179
Blemish, 42
Blend, 37, 136
blending, 109, 147, 164, 165
blocky, 126
blooming, 100, 101
blurriness, 100, 128, 132, 156, 180
borders, 102, 134, 153, 167, 180

boxes, 26, 46, 47, 77, 78, 91, 124, 143, 175
brightness, 22, 42, 66, 91, 92, 114, 118, 133, 141, 164
brush, 24, 36, 41, 82, 146, 153, 165, 170, 171, 184
Brush, 12, 14, 36, 37, 40, 41, 42, 163, 165, 170, 183, 184, 186
brushstrokes, 55, 74, 184
Burn, 42, 43

C

cacophony, 125
calendars, 153
camera, 27, 36, 59, 60, 64, 79, 81, 88, 97, 100, 102, 103, 105, 106, 118, 134, 137, 142
Camera, 5, 63, 64, 65, 66, 67, 104, 125
cameras, 63, 67, 70, 81, 96, 100, 111, 134
Cancel, 33, 66, 89
capabilities, 13, 14, 15, 24, 26, 28, 80, 139, 165, 167, 168
capability, 36, 47, 64, 66, 67, 164
capture, 63, 80, 100, 103, 111, 125, 131, 134
Capture, 14
Capturing, 79
cards, 153
catalog, 83, 84, 86
categories, 27, 84
category, 19, 32, 34, 161, 176

CD, 153
Center, 37, 38
Channel, 108, 114
checkbox, 20, 33, 37, 39, 48, 62, 66, 78, 82, 92, 93, 99, 108, 115, 124, 128, 130, 141, 142, 143, 145, 155, 156
chromatic, 100, 103
Chromatic, 100
clicking, 19, 31, 39, 41, 43, 46, 49, 54, 58, 68, 71, 81, 84, 86, 101, 112, 114, 151, 155, 158, 160, 161, 162, 179, 181, 183, 184
clipping, 20, 115
Clone, 40, 42
Cloning, 15
collection, 16, 27, 31, 67, 87, 155, 166
Collections, 27, 59, 83, 84, 85, 86, 87
color, 13, 14, 16, 20, 29, 34, 35, 41, 43, 49, 55, 57, 59, 60, 62, 66, 80, 90, 93, 94, 95, 96, 97, 99, 101, 103, 107, 108, 109, 114, 115, 116, 117, 118, 119, 120, 121, 122, 123, 124, 125, 126, 127, 128, 133, 134, 135, 138, 144, 145, 146, 147, 149, 150, 151, 153, 157, 158, 159, 165, 166, 174, 178, 179, 180, 181, 183, 184, 185, 186
Color, 4, 5, 8, 10, 11, 12, 34, 35, 43, 47, 49, 57, 58, 59, 108, 109, 114, 115, 121, 146, 147, 150, 156, 157, 158, 174, 176, 178, 179, 180, 181, 183, 184, 186
colors, 37, 42, 43, 47, 56, 74, 92, 93, 100, 103, 107, 115, 121, 122, 123, 124, 125, 138, 144, 149, 151, 157, 174
command, 35, 38, 46, 47, 53, 54, 60, 70, 75, 76, 77, 78, 79, 89, 90, 96, 97, 119, 121, 126, 129, 136, 137, 138, 139
commands, 29, 31, 39, 46, 53, 70, 75, 76, 127, 129, 133, 134, 135
comparison, 15, 63, 126, 142
compatibility, 16, 17, 169, 172
Complete, 16, 20, 26, 27, 32, 33, 84
completion, 37
composite, 14, 20, 114
compositions, 13
comprehensive, 15, 26, 27, 37, 53, 138, 168
computation, 126, 185
conduct, 33, 49, 86, 165, 168
configuration, 26, 33, 47, 66, 71, 75, 78, 92, 110, 112, 124, 131, 142, 161, 170, 171
configurations, 37, 46, 47, 57, 64, 67, 79, 81, 89, 91, 92, 110, 125, 156, 166
Configure, 89
contains, 16, 29, 31, 40, 90, 103, 179
Content, 15
contribute, 100

control, 49, 57, 58, 72, 74, 78, 79, 92, 93, 94, 95, 101, 105, 106, 108, 109, 112, 113, 114, 116, 117, 120, 121, 123, 124, 127, 128, 130, 131, 136, 137, 141, 156, 168, 182, 183, 184, 185

controllers, 35

controls, 20, 21, 26, 31, 47, 75, 80, 81, 89, 90, 92, 99, 102, 103, 108, 115, 116, 122, 141, 154, 155, 178, 179, 181, 184, 185

Corel, 1, 13, 14, 15, 16, 17, 19, 22, 23, 64, 67, 102, 131, 133, 135, 142, 144, 157, 158, 161, 162, 163, 165, 166, 167, 168, 169, 170, 171, 172, 173, 174, 186

correction, 16, 20, 79, 89, 90, 99, 101, 102, 103, 104, 116, 131, 135

Correction, 13, 42, 88, 89, 102, 103, 105, 106, 109, 131

corresponding, 19, 49, 51, 77, 93, 108, 115, 116, 124, 132, 159, 174, 175, 180

covers, 137, 153

creation, 13, 39, 60, 64, 124, 157, 161, 164, 166, 180

Crop, 22, 40, 42, 89

cursor, 29, 45, 46, 48, 53, 73, 82, 83, 115, 146, 159

customizable, 22, 36, 55, 149

Customization, 82

customized, 40, 157, 162

D

deactivate, 35, 73, 143

decrease, 60, 61, 92, 94, 124, 132, 154, 156, 169

Delete, 49, 93, 126, 149, 169

denotes, 103, 110, 126, 144, 156

design, 13, 15, 34, 56, 60, 144, 147, 153, 156, 157

Despeckle, 129

details, 2, 26, 27, 36, 38, 60, 71, 86, 126, 128, 129, 135, 136, 137, 143, 186

Determine, 101, 127, 129, 130

Determining, 55, 143

digital, 2, 13, 15, 20, 42, 60, 63, 66, 70, 79, 95, 96, 97, 100, 111, 120, 126, 134, 161

dimensions, 29, 34, 38, 45, 53, 61, 71, 90, 106, 132, 137, 138, 139, 140, 141, 142, 143, 161, 169, 180

directives, 28, 29, 74

discovery, 27

distinct, 15, 42, 46, 67, 100, 124, 125, 126, 128, 135, 144, 162, 165, 178, 179

distinguishes, 120, 126

distinguishing, 31

distorted, 42, 105

distortion, 13, 88, 102, 103, 104, 105, 120, 142

disturbance, 125, 129

docked, 35, 38

Dodge, 42

dragging, 38, 40, 42, 43, 44, 45, 53, 74, 90, 101, 109, 115, 124, 132, 139, 180, 183, 184
Dropper, 41, 115, 145, 146
DVD, 18

E

Edge, 129, 164, 165
Edit, 3, 4, 24, 28, 32, 38, 39, 40, 44, 45, 48, 49, 50, 55, 64, 65, 67, 70, 76, 79, 80, 91, 117, 118, 122, 131
edition, 14
editor, 13, 68, 151
effects, 13, 22, 29, 31, 37, 38, 42, 47, 61, 74, 102, 118, 120, 147, 166, 167, 175, 176, 177, 180
Effects, 21, 24, 29, 31, 34, 37, 38, 81, 175, 176, 178, 179, 181, 182, 183, 184, 185
efficiency, 27, 161, 162
Elevating, 156, 181
eliminate, 42, 126, 133, 150
elimination, 128, 129
enhancing, 13, 14, 30, 39, 42, 167, 168
enlarged, 82, 102, 118, 138, 141
eradicate, 128
Essentials, 14, 16, 20, 26
execution, 36, 37, 39, 74, 75
EXIF, 28, 37, 60, 86

F

facilitate, 15, 16, 29, 31, 37, 46, 68, 157, 166, 181
features, 14, 15, 17, 26, 33, 47, 80, 95, 162, 169
Files, 6, 29, 68, 69
Fill, 43, 94, 95, 112, 113, 145, 146, 148, 152, 154, 155
film, 22, 100, 126, 134, 167
Fix, 21, 46, 90, 91, 92, 111
Focus, 14, 46, 92, 132
folder, 27, 59, 62, 68, 83, 84, 85, 86, 152, 153, 157, 159, 162
foreground, 41, 43, 145, 146, 151, 153, 155, 160
Frame, 14, 15, 20, 44
Freehand, 41, 132, 163
fresh, 27, 85, 150, 159, 164, 170
function, 16, 21, 34, 40, 41, 43, 61, 71, 75, 76, 78, 81, 91, 100, 101, 114, 126, 128, 130, 134, 138, 164, 178, 180, 182, 185
functions, 16, 17, 40, 64, 111, 128

G

gallery, 80
General, 55, 62, 78, 141
generate, 20, 28, 37, 101, 107, 118, 121, 147, 149, 155, 163, 164, 176, 177, 178, 186
Gradient, 43, 148, 149, 150, 151, 152, 153, 156

Gradually, 128
granted, 157, 164
graph, 99, 111, 114, 115, 117, 118
graphic, 13, 161, 166
graphical, 36
graphics, 153, 169, 171
green, 36, 96, 99, 107, 109, 114, 121, 123, 125, 144
grids, 55
group, 44, 57, 62, 92, 99, 105, 106, 108, 115, 117, 124
guide, 20, 22, 55, 57, 58, 59, 168
guidelines, 55, 86, 107, 110
guides, 55
Guides, 5, 55, 58, 59

H

hardware, 34
histogram, 20, 110, 111, 114, 115, 116, 117, 118
horizontal, 53, 55, 57, 58, 90, 111, 118, 180
hues, 20, 56, 93, 96, 106, 107, 120, 121, 135, 138, 145, 147, 149, 150, 151, 154, 157, 165, 179, 185

I

icon, 13, 16, 20, 27, 31, 32, 33, 38, 45, 46, 47, 49, 51, 52, 65, 66, 67, 68, 74, 75, 76, 77, 79, 81, 83, 87, 115, 116, 124, 142, 145, 146, 147, 148, 149, 151, 154, 155, 156, 158, 159, 160, 161, 165, 178

iconography, 33
illuminated, 66, 113, 118, 181, 183, 184
illustrate, 36, 99, 107, 166
image, 5, 13, 14, 15, 22, 23, 26, 27, 29, 31, 34, 35, 36, 37, 39, 40, 42, 43, 44, 47, 48, 49, 50, 51, 52, 53, 54, 55, 57, 59, 60, 61, 63, 64, 65, 66, 67, 68, 69, 70, 71, 72, 73, 74, 75, 77, 78, 79, 80, 81, 82, 83, 85, 87, 89, 90, 91, 93, 94, 95, 96, 97, 99, 100, 101, 102, 103, 104, 105, 106, 107, 108, 109, 110, 111, 112, 113, 114, 115, 116, 117, 118, 119, 120, 121, 122, 124, 125, 126, 128, 129, 130, 133, 134, 135, 136, 137, 138, 139, 141, 142, 143, 145, 146, 152, 153, 154, 155, 156, 157, 161, 163, 164, 165, 167, 168, 169, 172, 173, 176, 177, 178, 179, 180, 181, 182, 183, 184, 185, 186
Image, 4, 5, 6, 7, 9, 10, 24, 47, 48, 50, 51, 52, 53, 59, 73, 74, 86, 90, 95, 99, 107, 115, 121, 129, 134, 139, 142, 145, 154, 176, 179
images, 15, 16, 20, 26, 28, 29, 30, 31, 36, 39, 40, 42, 43, 44, 46, 49, 55, 59, 60, 61, 62, 64, 66, 67, 70, 71, 78, 79, 80, 83, 84, 85, 86, 92, 93, 95, 96, 97, 100, 101, 102, 104, 107, 110, 118, 119, 133, 134, 135, 136, 137, 142, 143,

144, 161, 164, 166, 167, 168, 173, 176, 177, 186
increases, 95, 121, 156, 181, 182, 185
indicated, 73, 78, 83, 117, 132, 183, 184
indispensable, 30, 153, 163
information, 26, 27, 33, 37, 39, 60, 68, 69, 81, 83, 84, 85, 103, 113, 118, 126, 138, 182
installation, 16, 17, 19, 170
Instant, 21, 22, 31, 34, 37, 81, 175, 176
instructions, 19, 20, 35, 38, 70, 74, 75, 79, 127
instrument, 33, 39, 80, 156
instruments, 15, 26, 28, 31, 33, 39, 40, 165, 170
integration, 42
integrity, 126, 129, 150
interface, 13, 16, 24, 36, 39, 45, 53, 62, 68, 80, 81, 83, 90, 145, 155, 159, 160, 171, 176
interfaces, 82
interruptions, 17, 162

J

JPEG, 60, 62, 63, 64, 67, 104, 125, 126, 142

K

known, 20, 21, 46, 165, 178

L

Layer, 7, 90, 164, 165
luminance, 36, 42, 94, 108, 110, 114, 117, 120, 121, 124, 126, 133, 137, 181, 185
luminosity, 13, 43, 92, 107, 110, 117, 118, 124, 182, 183, 185

M

Magic, 41, 163
magnification, 37, 50, 71, 72, 73, 99, 100, 102, 112, 114
magnifier, 73
Magnifier, 73
magnitude, 42, 101, 104, 154, 156, 180, 184
malfunctions, 96, 125
manipulating, 36, 45, 82, 121, 134
Manually, 18, 110, 124
Material, 152, 154, 155, 157
Max, 118
Menu, 5, 29, 54
midtones, 36, 118
miniature, 34, 40
minimal, 17, 26
minimum, 55, 100, 109, 113, 118, 128, 129, 130, 137, 169
Mixer, 37, 108
mode, 14, 24, 49, 60, 63, 67, 73, 80, 82, 104, 111, 136, 145, 167

modification, 15, 16, 22, 26, 29, 33, 37, 39, 42, 47, 60, 88, 114, 151, 161, 171, 181, 183, 186
modifications, 30, 33, 47, 50, 52, 57, 64, 66, 67, 68, 74, 78, 80, 81, 91, 105, 106, 108, 114, 116, 121, 125, 150, 164, 168, 174
Modifications, 6, 48, 81, 118
modify, 28, 35, 37, 38, 43, 44, 45, 46, 49, 52, 55, 62, 66, 67, 68, 74, 78, 80, 81, 82, 90, 91, 92, 94, 95, 99, 104, 105, 106, 110, 111, 112, 114, 115, 116, 117, 118, 121, 122, 123, 124, 128, 132, 133, 138, 140, 141, 142, 143, 146, 149, 150, 152, 154, 156, 161, 162, 163, 164, 168, 171, 181, 185, 186
Moire, 128, 129
Move, 4, 40, 41, 45, 146
MultiCam, 14
multitude, 28, 79, 87, 100, 161, 171

N

Navigate, 52, 54, 57, 61, 66, 68, 69, 71, 74, 81, 99, 121, 124, 129, 130, 131, 153, 154, 156, 184
navigating, 46, 57, 59, 89, 156, 157, 159
Navigation, 59, 82, 83, 84, 85, 86
neighbors, 126

Noise, 8, 9, 66, 96, 97, 99, 125, 127, 128, 129, 130, 131
numerals, 56
numerous, 16, 37, 84, 111, 123, 125, 154, 162, 185

O

Objects, 14
online, 60, 153
opacity, 83, 150, 151, 171, 178, 180, 185
operations, 20, 29, 31, 36, 74, 77, 78, 79, 82, 100, 107, 110, 162, 166, 181, 183
option, 16, 17, 21, 25, 26, 33, 39, 47, 52, 56, 59, 61, 62, 63, 65, 66, 68, 69, 71, 72, 73, 74, 75, 77, 78, 81, 82, 85, 87, 89, 90, 92, 93, 98, 102, 106, 107, 109, 115, 117, 122, 123, 124, 127, 128, 131, 136, 140, 141, 142, 143, 146, 150, 156, 157, 158, 160, 161, 164, 170, 171, 174, 178, 179, 181, 182, 185, 186
organizer, 28, 37
Organizer, 27, 31, 37, 53, 54, 59, 65, 68, 80, 81, 82, 83, 84, 85
organizing, 27, 35, 84
outcomes, 21, 37, 75, 121, 129, 166

P

Painter, 14

painting, 36, 37, 39, 42, 153
Paintshop, 15, 16
PaintShop, 1, 13, 14, 15, 16, 17, 19, 20, 21, 22, 23, 26, 32, 35, 46, 53, 59, 60, 61, 64, 67, 71, 80, 86, 95, 96, 102, 104, 107, 110, 111, 120, 125, 127, 131, 133, 135, 137, 142, 144, 145, 152, 153, 155, 156, 157, 158, 159, 161, 162, 163, 165, 166, 167, 168, 169, 170, 171, 172, 173, 174, 177, 186
palette, 20, 27, 31, 34, 35, 36, 37, 38, 44, 45, 46, 50, 53, 54, 56, 57, 59, 65, 74, 75, 76, 77, 80, 82, 83, 84, 85, 86, 89, 148, 151, 155, 157, 158, 159, 160, 175, 176
Palettes, 7, 11, 20, 29, 35, 37, 44, 83, 111, 158
Pan, 4, 6, 40, 47, 48, 53, 73, 74, 101
pane, 32, 38, 39, 40, 48, 49, 51, 55, 59, 64, 65, 66, 67, 69, 80, 82, 83, 84, 87, 91, 93, 99, 100, 101, 109, 115, 122, 128, 146, 152, 159, 176, 181, 184
panel, 21, 59, 72, 74, 78, 81, 83, 86, 89, 90, 115, 145, 146, 152, 153, 156, 158, 159, 160, 165
panes, 47, 50, 100, 112, 114, 116, 117
parameter, 47, 103, 104, 105, 129, 141, 181, 182, 183
parameters, 33, 36, 37, 47, 49, 62, 67, 68, 90, 92, 97, 99, 103, 104, 109, 113, 122, 124, 141, 146, 152, 156, 164, 171, 173, 174, 175, 176, 180
particles, 126, 129, 130, 151
Pattern, 10, 128, 129, 154, 156
patterns, 14, 126, 128, 131, 153, 155, 157
Patterns, 9, 128, 153
pavement, 155
Pen, 40, 44
percentages, 13
performance, 14, 17, 34, 169
permissions, 17
Perspective, 7, 42, 88, 89, 90
photo, 13, 15, 16, 22, 23, 27, 31, 36, 66, 68, 69, 80, 90, 92, 93, 134, 186
Photo, 21, 24, 46, 90, 91, 92, 111
photograph, 20, 21, 22, 24, 27, 31, 95, 97, 100, 105, 107, 110, 116, 137
photographs, 13, 15, 16, 21, 37, 38, 39, 42, 50, 60, 61, 67, 80, 86, 87, 90, 93, 95, 97, 102, 120, 125, 126, 136, 137, 164, 166, 167, 174
photography, 26, 33, 34, 60, 93, 96
Photography, 16, 20, 24, 26, 32, 33
photos, 27, 32, 39, 67, 71, 84
pigments, 37
pixels, 13, 41, 43, 55, 58, 93, 101, 105, 110, 111, 117, 118, 119, 121, 125, 126, 127, 128, 130, 133, 134, 135, 136, 137, 138, 140, 141, 142, 143, 145, 178, 181, 182

PlayStation, 16
Portable, 16
possibility, 154
practical, 13, 38, 162
preconfigured, 26
predetermined, 41, 55
preferences, 14, 26, 66, 82, 83, 162, 163, 170, 171
Preferences, 55, 62, 78, 141, 159, 163
present, 26, 34, 36, 40, 42, 47, 68, 84, 93, 101, 108, 111, 117, 126, 137, 141, 143, 169, 185
presentation, 70, 156
Presenting, 37, 41, 156
presets, 13, 116, 166, 176, 177
preview, 22, 27, 34, 47, 66, 74, 82, 155, 156
Preview, 4, 7, 31, 47, 48, 53, 66, 82, 87, 115
Previews, 47
print, 13, 37, 142, 173, 174
Pro, 1, 13, 14, 15, 16, 17, 19, 20, 26, 32, 35, 46, 53, 59, 60, 61, 64, 67, 71, 80, 86, 95, 96, 102, 104, 107, 110, 111, 120, 125, 127, 131, 133, 135, 137, 142, 144, 145, 152, 153, 155, 156, 157, 158, 161, 162, 163, 165, 166, 167, 168, 169, 170, 171, 172, 173, 174, 177, 186
problematic, 129, 130
procedure, 17, 19, 23, 59, 69, 79, 84, 97, 128

productivity, 13, 70, 71, 162
products, 153, 174
professionals, 13, 60
program, 14, 15, 16, 19, 20, 23, 59, 60, 71, 74, 99, 126, 144, 167, 168, 172, 173, 186
Program, 55, 62, 78, 141
programs, 17, 145
Programs, 19
project, 27
projects, 13, 153, 157
promotional, 26
Properties, 5, 56, 90, 148, 152, 153, 154, 155, 157
prototype, 14
punctuation, 56

R

RAW, 5, 6, 60, 63, 64, 65, 66, 67, 68, 69, 104
recently, 27, 62, 74, 75, 80, 148, 155, 176
rectification, 42
Red, 42, 46, 103, 108, 109, 114
Refined, 15
reflected, 48, 72, 99
regions, 13, 42, 66, 81, 82, 93, 94, 95, 97, 101, 109, 110, 113, 115, 120, 126, 131, 134, 147, 163, 164, 165
reinstate, 128
remember, 38, 53, 71, 142

Removal, 8, 42, 46, 96, 97, 99, 100, 127, 128, 129
remove, 84, 87, 89, 93, 102, 107, 115, 126, 141, 149
Remove, 7, 9, 10, 82, 85, 87, 99, 115, 127, 128, 129, 130, 131, 149
Remover, 13, 42
renders, 13, 93
repairing, 13, 134
Replacement, 14, 23
replete, 26
representation, 36, 50, 120, 124, 154, 174
reshaping, 41
resize, 50, 53, 139, 141, 162
resizing, 13, 38, 44, 71, 83, 139, 140, 141
resolves, 42, 171
restoring, 13
retouching, 37, 167
reverse, 36, 74, 75, 76, 77, 82
rotation, 22, 41, 124, 181, 183, 184
routine, 38
rulers, 55, 57
runs, 17

S

Scratch, 13, 42
script, 36, 37, 39, 79, 177, 180
scroll, 53, 72
segmented, 27, 36
selecting, 16, 20, 24, 27, 32, 33, 35, 39, 40, 41, 43, 46, 47, 49, 51, 52, 53, 54, 57, 59, 62, 65, 66, 68, 71, 72, 74, 75, 77, 78, 79, 80, 81, 82, 84, 85, 90, 91, 96, 99, 103, 106, 108, 111, 117, 118, 122, 124, 125, 127, 128, 130, 136, 142, 144, 146, 150, 151, 152,153, 156, 157, 159, 160, 161, 170, 178, 179, 181, 182, 183, 184
selection, 13, 24, 29, 30, 40, 41, 43, 47, 48, 49, 56, 82, 92, 103, 110, 114, 120, 124, 130, 131, 132, 133, 134, 135, 139, 146, 151, 163, 164, 165, 166, 178, 179, 180, 182, 186
Selection, 10, 15, 41, 81, 82, 132, 154, 163, 165, 166
selections, 47, 55, 163
Selective, 46
Sensor, 100
settings, 27, 34, 36, 42, 46, 47, 49, 57, 62, 66, 67, 68, 92, 97, 103, 108, 116, 118, 136, 137, 145, 166, 170, 171, 176, 178, 179, 180
Setup, 18
shape, 20, 41, 44, 89, 131, 163, 181, 182
sharing, 16, 60, 135
Show, 4, 37, 47, 59, 76
sketching, 37
slider, 21, 49, 66, 82, 92, 93, 94, 95, 98, 107, 108, 117, 118, 123, 124, 129, 132, 143
Smart, 21, 41, 42, 46, 86, 87, 90, 91, 92, 107, 111, 165, 166

smooth, 134, 165
Smooth, 129, 131, 176
snap, 55, 57
Snap, 14, 57, 90
software, 13, 14, 15, 16, 17, 41, 42, 59, 60, 61, 70, 96, 103, 126, 152, 162, 168, 169, 170, 172, 173, 174, 186
Software, 16
solutions, 13, 142, 174
space, 47, 61, 78, 117, 150, 179
Spacebar, 53, 74
Special, 70, 138, 139
spectrum, 34, 101, 110, 119, 126
speed, 13, 78, 134
Stacking, 14
Standard, 33, 39, 62, 76, 79
status, 29, 38, 39
storage, 62, 78, 157
Straighten, 42
stratum, 138, 164
streamlined, 17, 33
Strength, 94, 95, 98, 104, 105, 106, 113, 176
stroke, 41, 43, 184
Stroke, 148, 153, 155, 184
supplementary, 2, 38, 91
symmetric, 20

T

tasks, 26, 39, 40, 144, 162
taxing, 79
telephoto, 100

temperature, 107, 108
temporarily, 34
Text, 20, 40, 44
texture, 42, 125, 126, 127, 144, 154, 155, 156, 157, 165
texture's, 155, 156
thumbnail, 34, 37, 50, 54, 65, 67, 68, 69, 80, 82, 154, 157, 177
thumbnails, 27, 31, 37, 65, 68, 69, 84, 157, 161
tool, 13, 15, 16, 20, 22, 23, 29, 35, 36, 37, 40, 41, 42, 53, 66, 72, 73, 74, 81, 88, 89, 90, 146, 152, 156, 163, 164, 166, 171
Tool, 10, 12, 14, 15, 20, 37, 44, 72, 74, 89, 145, 163, 166, 170, 180, 186
toolbar, 20, 28, 31, 33, 34, 39, 40, 42, 45, 46, 54, 72, 73, 76, 79, 81, 83, 152, 180
toolbars, 26, 29, 35, 38, 39, 44, 45, 56, 162
Toolbars, 29, 39
tools, 13, 15, 22, 23, 26, 27, 28, 30, 31, 33, 37, 39, 40, 42, 53, 60, 67, 80, 83, 84, 86, 96, 132, 146, 156, 162, 163, 164, 165, 166, 167, 168, 174, 186
tooltip, 38, 159
Toothbrush, 42
Traditional, 16
transform, 119, 121, 154
transformed, 20, 75

U

underexposed, 93, 111
undertones, 125
Uninstall, 19
uninstalling, 20
update, 14, 68, 115
upgraded, 15
users, 16, 17, 20, 26, 27, 33, 64, 72, 75, 86, 92, 111, 145, 153, 162, 163, 164, 166, 177

V

Variance, 36
variety, 22, 26, 29, 35, 40, 42, 71, 92, 125, 139, 144, 145, 153, 156, 162, 164, 166, 176, 178
various, 13, 24, 47, 49, 50, 60, 102, 125, 133, 138, 139, 153, 154, 166
vector, 20, 40, 41, 53, 152
versatile, 13, 161
vertical, 52, 53, 55, 58, 90, 111, 118, 180
vignette, 102, 103, 167
visibility, 28, 45, 46, 71, 83, 90, 125, 128, 145, 179, 181

W

Wand, 41, 163
Welcome, 3, 20, 26, 32
Windows, 5, 16, 17, 19, 46, 52, 59, 70, 145
workspace, 20, 24, 26, 27, 28, 32, 33, 34, 44, 71, 162, 171
Workspace, 12, 15, 16, 20, 34, 35, 162, 171
workspaces, 16, 20, 21, 26, 32, 34

Z

zoom, 71, 100, 101, 116, 117, 128
Zoom, 6, 40, 47, 53, 72, 73, 74, 128

Printed in Great Britain
by Amazon